Tchaikovsky in America

WITHDRAWN
UTSA LIBRARIES

TCHAIKOVSKY

IN AMERICA

THE COMPOSER'S VISIT IN 1891

ELKHONON YOFFE

Translations from Russian by LIDYA YOFFE

NEW YORK   OXFORD

Oxford University Press

1986

Oxford University Press

Oxford New York Toronto
Delhi Bombay Calcutta Madras Karachi
Petaling Jaya Singapore Hong Kong Tokyo
Nairobi Dar es Salaam Cape Town
Melbourne Auckland

and associated companies in
Beirut Berlin Ibadan Nicosia

Copyright © 1986 by Elkhonon Yoffe

Published by Oxford University Press, Inc.,
200 Madison Avenue, New York, New York 10016

Oxford is a registered trademark of Oxford University Press

All rights reserved. No part of this publication may be reproduced,
stored in a retrieval system, or transmitted, in any form or by any means,
electronic, mechanical, photocopying, recording, or otherwise,
without the prior permission of Oxford University Press.

Library of Congress Cataloging-in-Publication Data
Yoffe, Elkhonon.
Tchaikovsky in America.
Based on Tchaikovsky's diaries.
Includes index.
1. Tchaikovsky, Peter Ilich, 1840–1893.
2. Composers—Soviet Union—Biography. 3. Tchaikovsky,
Peter Ilich, 1840–1893—Journeys—United States.
I. Yoffe, Lidya. II. Tchaikovsky, Peter Ilich,
1840–1893. Dnevniki. III. Title.
ML410.C4Y63 1986 780'.92'4 [B] 86-8785
ISBN 0-19-504117-8

9 8 7 6 5 4 3 2 1
Printed in the United States of America

LIBRARY
The University of Texas
At San Antonio

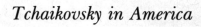

Tchaikovsky in America

Preface

In the early '70s of the last century, more than a hundred years ago, music by Tchaikovsky was heard for the first time in America. Almost immediately he became one of the most beloved and oft-performed composers in this country. Owing to some strange turn of fate Tchaikovsky's musical career in this country developed more happily than in Russia.[1] This is a paradox. But Tchaikovsky's life was full of paradoxes. He himself sensed this peculiarity and, being aware of the spread of his artistic fortune overseas, was quite interested in the country where he had achieved such unexpected recognition. By the time of his visit to America in the spring of 1891 his American fame had attained great scope, as he learned upon his arrival. With feelings of pride mixed with bitterness he wrote from New York to his nephew Vladimir Davidov on April 30, 1891: "It turns out that I am ten times better known in America than in Europe. At first when they told me that, I thought that it was an exaggerated compliment, but now I see that it is the truth. Works of mine that are still unknown in Moscow, are performed here several times a season, and whole reviews and commentaries are written on them (e.g., *Hamlet*). I am far more of a big shot here than in Russia. Is it not curious!!!" It is curious, too, that certain of his best works, such as the Piano Concerto No. 1 and the Violin Concerto, were performed for the first time in America rather than in his homeland, Russia, or in Europe, from whence his music usually came.

The romance between Tchaikovsky and America, which began so successfully so long ago, continues now and has by no means dwindled. During past years his music and especially his instrumental works have become an integral part of the musical culture of America. His compositions appear regularly in symphony and chamber concerts, opera and ballet theaters, in concerts for children and young people, even in symphony "pops" concerts; entire programmes are built from his works; festivals of Tchaikovsky's music take place. Then there are the Tchaikovsky marathons, these events purely American in their scope, in which the music of different genres is performed for an entire day or even two to three days, with only the musicians and listeners changing. The tradition of performing Tchaikovsky's *Nutcracker* every Christmas in cities throughout the land is quite unique. It is safe to say that nothing of the kind exists anywhere else in the world.

Tchaikovsky's brief visit to America in the spring of 1891 was without doubt the culmination of the composer's popularity in this country at that time. After a century this visit may seem to be a small speck in the history of America, but it is endowed with symbolic importance and creates a unique spiritual proximity for the relationship between America and Tchaikovsky. The fact that Tchaikovsky came in person to America, that just he was chosen for the opening of the famous Carnegie Hall, without which the history of the American musical life would be different, gives a special flavor to America's love of the music of Tchaikovsky. It is as though Tchaikovsky blessed the country and its love for music.

A great amount of thoroughly interesting documentary material for this event remains: Tchaikovsky's letters and detailed diaries; newspaper and magazine articles and reviews of his stay and performances conducted; interviews; letters from his friends and American acquaintances; recollections of his contemporaries; and other materials. And yet Tchaikovsky's journey overseas has never been given within literature the attention it deserves. Indeed there are no publications that place an accent on this historic contact between Tchaikovsky and America. It is true that all the biographies published in English contain more or less detailed descriptions of the event. As a rule the authors use some of the documents but mostly limit themselves by retelling the story with a few excerpts. The visit is simply presented as one of Tchaikovsky's many foreign tours, if slightly more poignant for the composer. Some authors especially like to accentuate Tchaikovsky's fierce homesickness and despair, so the visit seems almost a total calamity (E. W. Schallenbern, *Tchaikovsky*; Edwin Evans, *Tchaikovsky*; John Gee, *The Triumph of Tchaikovsky*). Even among the books that present Tchaikovsky's visit in more detail and impartially there is no attempt to see more than bare facts (H. Winstock, *Tchaikovsky*; R. Schickel, *The World of Carnegie Hall*).

Books published within the Soviet Union merely mention the visit in passing, or provide details in the form of specially adjusted quotations from Tchaikovsky's letters and diaries, with excessive authorial comment. The composer is pictured almost as a "Soviet man," a "Party functionary," who solemnly and with a "class dignity" struts about the streets of American cities turning contemptuously aside from "the sham charms of American prosperity" (A. Stoiko, *The Great Composer*; V. Kholodkovsky, *A House in Klin*). As a single exception there is Alexandra Orlova's *About Music, Life, Myself*, in which Tchaikovsky's visit is discussed more objectively.

Based entirely on documentary material that relates to Tchaikovsky's visit, the present book unfolds for the first time the whole story behind the event, beginning with Tchaikovsky's initial invitation to come to America and ending with the negotiations for a second tour, which began after his return to Russia and continued almost until the very death of the composer on November 6, 1893. This book presents

Tchaikovsky as seen by Americans, and America through Tchaikovsky's eyes. Above all it tells the story of the highly dramatic last years of the great Russian composer's life. The letters and diaries of Tchaikovsky included in this book are newly translated into English; a number of letters are translated for the first time. We have faithfully followed the originals. The index of names provides short identifications.

The author expresses his profound gratitude for the invaluable help in the creation of this book to his beloved wife, adviser, and translator, Lidya Yoffe; to his son Mark, for his creative ideas and help; to David Haas, the editor of translations; and also to Marianne Haddock, Natalie Chalis, Gregory Kuperstein, and Rich and Kay Hancock.

June 1986   E.Y.

Contents

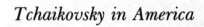

Tchaikovsky in America

Introduction

by ANTAL DORATI

An introduction to a book must neither be a critical essay—because it is to be read before the book itself—nor a publicity "blurb"—that is taken care of by the publisher—and least of all should not reveal too much of the book's content, and thus take the wind out of the author's sails.

What, then, should an introduction be?

The best way to look at it, would be, perhaps, as an "appetizer."

In the case of the present publication that is hardly necessary, for its title alone kindles enough curiosity. However, as it is well known, the role of the appetizer is not so much to fill a need as to be agreeable and, so one hopes, stimulating.

This is, then, also the intent of the following few lines written during a musing hour, after having been intensely engrossed in reading the manuscript.

The documents—letters, diaries, and press clippings—that Mr. Elkhonon Yoffe compiled and has modestly, I might say, reverently, brought into context with his own, sparsely interposed text, all pertaining to the Russian master's only trip to the United States in 1891, make indeed very interesting reading. They fascinated me for a number of reasons, transcending the curiosity of the musician by what they reveal.

In my many years of reading experience so far I have seldom come across a so intimately detailed account of so interesting a subject as this visit of a great European composer to the shores of America. That the great European artist should be a Russian, a real Russian from head to toe—adds special flavor to the story, especially for the American reader of today.

It is no news that musicians, since the time of the troubadours (or even earlier?), have always been a traveling lot. Nowadays they travel in ever increasing measure, as travel becomes easier and faster with the times.

In the case of performing musicians the traveling "mania" can be readily understood; less so in the case of composers, for traveling per se is counterproductive to creative work. That "one has to see the world" in order to write about it, that one has to live through the passions one is setting into sounds of music, is simply not true: creative "seeing" and "living" happens in the fantasy. For a composer it is best if he sits at home and composes.

This is, also, what usually happens. Composers' trips are relatively rare, and thus are also more remarkable and interesting in their effect upon the traveler and upon the new environments they visit.

But it is astonishing how little we know, in general, of these episodes.

We possess precious records of Joseph Haydn's two trips to London in the 1790s. Of Mozart's many voyages we know much less, hardly more than their itinerary. Neither composer ever expressed a desire to travel across the Atlantic. Mozart's librettist, da Ponte, however, did come to the United States—true, long after Mozart's death—and stayed there until the end of his life.

In our own time the United States is playing an ever increasing role in the lives—and work—of European music makers. Practically every one of them travels extensively to and within the U.S. To cite only a few of the most remarkable "imports," or "transplants" in this field, let us remember that Puccini composed his "La Fanciulla del West" for the Metropolitan Opera House of New York, that Rachmaninoff made his home in the U.S., that Milhaud and Dallapiccola taught in American universities, and Stravinsky and Schonberg settled in California.

Around, roughly, the 1850s a most interesting project loomed in the world of music, that came to naught: Richard Wagner was tempted and contemplated for a while moving to America. If that plan would have come through, at least the geographic aspect of music history would have considerably changed, with a possible Bayreuth in Kentucky or thereabouts.

In the 1890s three very great European composers visited the New World. They were, in short succession: Tchaikovsky, Dvořák, and Johann Strauss.

Biographies of these musicians, of course, duly record their American visits—in Dvořák's case this was a lengthier stay, during which two great masterpieces (the Ninth Symphony and the cello concerto) were born—but, as I said already, to my knowledge special studies of these events—dramatic rencontres as they were—have not as yet been made.

Yet it is of great interest to explore these movements of human interreactions in depth, and not only for the information they give of the personality—and artistry—of the composer in question.

As one reader of the documents that follow here, I was struck by the revelations they contain about the reaction and behavior of the Americans toward a famous European suddenly appearing in their midst.

For they are not the same kind of people.

Since the first landing of Europeans on the shores of the New World, one can say—indeed one should say and recognize the fact—that a new type, a new kind of "white man" has evolved.

The difference between the new- and the old-world man became, during the intervening centuries, larger and larger, in about the same measure by which the distance between the two continents has shrunk. (Let's compare the voyage of the *Santa Maria* with that of a Concorde, to clarify what I mean.)

Speaking as a European who lived about one half of his life in the New World—became what could be called a somewhat useful member of it—and at least once a year still goes back and forth across the Atlantic Ocean, I can say that the difference between the two continents is enormous, and does not begin, but ends with the differences of their peoples. Indeed, the very air one breathes is different (I compare the pure, unpolluted air of the two lands, wherever that still can be found), the light has different shades, the winds blow differently, the same fruits are of different taste, the behavior of animals is not the same, and the people, we humans, *Homo sapiens*, of the same races living on the two continents, differ from each other most profoundly in the way we live, in the way we think, in the way we feel. (Also, of course, in the way we speak and write. To narrow the comparison to that of the English and the Americans, one can smilingly think of Winston Churchill's saying that they are divided, first by the Atlantic Ocean and, second, by the English language. No mere witticism this, but sharp and valid observation.)

The above is not said in complaint. Our unique planet is not made what it is by sameness but by the infinite variety of all things and beings existing on its surface and in its depths.

If I were to make a complaint—which is not the intent of this writing—it would be that we—humans—when dealing with each other are not reckoning with and are not respecting these differences in our respective natures. Our present-day international diplomacy especially shows a lamentable lack of sensitivity in this regard. As long as a respresentative of one nation thinks that his counterpart from another land is the same kind of person he is, there is no hope that they will understand each other.

The most sensitive creatures our earth has produced to

date are that special bread of the human race that is called the creative artist.

It is, thus, of particular interest, and it should be emphasized, not only for those who are concerned with the arts and with artists, but for everyone caring for humanity and humans, to learn how these hypersensitive minds and souls react to these intercontinental human differences, how they leave their mark on that other kind of people, and, in turn, how they are impressed and influenced by them.

Seldom, all too seldom, has this kind of meeting been recorded. And an even greater rarity is to find a record in which the human element lies naked, so to say, on the surface.

Reading Marco Polo's descriptions of his travels one has to dig deeply under the hard crust of the merchant to discover the human element, which, once laid bare, proves itself to be highly "romantic." In Goethe's "Italienische Reise" it is the sublimity of the writer's art that clouds the revelation of the artist's innermost secrets by giving the reader already sublimated and sublimely formulated material.

It is his "human material" that we see "laid out" before our very eyes, without any cover, bare and simple, deep and shallow, great and small, naive and *raffiné*—both as a unique piece of information to digest and to understand, and as a revelation of an overly sensitive, very tender human soul to cherish and to love.

Seen from the other end, as mirrored both in Tchaikovsky's diary and letters as well as in the wisely included clippings from American newspapers, it is especially touching how warmly the Terre Neuve (as Tchaikovsky himself liked to call America) has embraced the artist and instinctively felt his greatness, long before his native land came to honor him as was his due.

I

The Invitation

The story of Tchaikovsky's visit to America in the spring of 1891 begins roughly one year earlier, with a man named Walter Damrosch. In 1890 Damrosch was only twenty-eight years old but already one of the most brilliant and illustrious musical figures in New York. He was a well-known pianist, conductor, and head of the Oratorio Society and the New York Symphony Society, two prominent concert organizations of New York which he had led since the sudden death in 1885 of his father, Dr. Leopold Damrosch, who was their founder. He was also the associate conductor of the German Opera Company at the New York Metropolitan Opera. Although Walter Damrosch's early conducting appearances had not infrequently been the subject of criticism, none could deny his outstanding talent for organization. By 1890 he had attracted Andrew Carnegie, J. P. Morgan, John D. Rockefeller, Collis P. Huntington, three Vanderbilts, and various other wealthy patrons to serve on the Boards of the Oratorio Society and the New York Symphony Society, and he was married to the daughter of James G. Blaine, Secretary of State in President Benjamin Harrison's administration and one of the most influential men of his day.

Walter Damrosch was on particularly friendly terms with Andrew Carnegie, the great American iron master, writer, politician, and outstandingly generous philanthropist who founded many cultural institutions for the country such as schools, libraries, and museums. Walter Damrosch convinced Carnegie of the need for a new, large concert hall in New York. In 1889 Carnegie established the Music

*Hall Company and allotted two million dollars for the erection of
the Music Hall (later named Carnegie Hall). Design and construction of the hall were placed in the hands of the architect William
Burnet Tuthill, who was also a cellist, singer, and acoustician.*

*With his own characteristic verve and Carnegie's support, Walter
Damrosch made plans to celebrate the opening of the Hall with a
great Music Festival involving a large orchestra, a huge chorus, an
array of world-famous vocalists, and several United States premieres
of new music. But the central event was to be the participation of
the famous Russian composer Peter Ilyich Tchaikovsky, who was to
conduct several of his own compositions.*

*The invitation to Tchaikovsky was not a chance one. He was one
of the most eminent living composers and his music, especially his
symphonic and chamber music, had for the preceding ten years been
steadily increasing in fame and popularity throughout America. Walter
Damrosch was a great admirer of Tchaikovsky's music and had gladly
performed his compositions in concert, continuing the cause begun
by his father Leopold, who had been one of the first in America to
perform and popularize Tchaikovsky's music. By 1880 Leopold
Damrosch had already written the following to Tchaikovsky:*

New York, January 21, 1880

Dear Sir,

Let me take this opportunity to inform you that, having
received your new Suite Op. 43 [Suite No. 1] on the 10th
of this month, I have already performed it twice (once in
open rehearsal and once in concert), each time with great
success. The fanfare I received I promptly attributed to
you, the composer. Now I am pleased to report it to you.
Our performance, I'm bold enough to think, would have
been quite satisfying to you, for I omitted nothing at all, in
order that the work's multifarious charms be displayed.
The first movement, Divertissement and Scherzo were especially well-liked; the Gavotte, too, found many friends and
the Andantino even more.

Now I am looking forward to your new symphony [Symphony No. 4 in F Minor, Op. 36]! If I receive it in time I may yet perform it this winter. I am now an especially devoted admirer of your talent, a talent which, one hopes, will continue to grow.

Sincerely yours,
Leopold Damrosch

Allow me also to congratulate you on your magnificent Violin Concerto [Op. 35]. Is it not possible for the orchestral parts to appear any sooner?[2]

In order to establish a contact with Tchaikovsky, Walter Damrosch wrote to Herman Wolff, the head of the Berlin concert agency Musicwolff, who managed most of Tchaikovsky's foreign tours. In late September 1890, Tchaikovsky received a letter from Herman Wolff:

Berlin, September 20, 1890

My dear friend,

I had good news from America. My friend Damrosch writes that he hopes to arrange several concerts for you in the spring of 1891. He promised to provide details in three to four weeks.

Damrosch writes that they play a great deal of your music and respect you very much in America. I believe that the matter will soon be decided and that I will soon assist with your American triumph.

Wait for my report. I congratulate you for the time being.

Hermann Wolff

What new music have you written?

Meanwhile Tchaikovsky was living in the village Frolovskoe, which is near Klin, a small town in the province of Moscow (fifty miles northwest of Moscow), where he had rented a house with a large orchard from a local landowner. With him lived his valet Alexey Sofronov, who supervised household affairs. The composer had recently returned from St. Petersburg, where The Queen of Spades, an opera he loved dearly and considered to be his best, had gone off with great success (December 9, 1890). Now he was occupied with finishing music for a production of Shakespeare's Hamlet, commissioned by the Petersburg Dramatic Theater. The work was difficult and thoroughly exhausted him. Simultaneously he had begun work on a two-act ballet Casse-noisette (The Nutcracker), based on E. T. A. Hoffmann's tale, and a one-act opera, King René's Daughter (Iolanthe), taken from Henrik Hertz's play, both of which had been requested by the Directorate of the Imperial Theater for the season of 1891–92. He also corresponded regularly with a great number of people. Sometimes a small circle of friends or relatives would come to see him; at other times he would make short trips to Moscow or St. Petersburg.

It was just about this time when the composer was disposed more and more to periods of emotional weariness and was preyed upon by doubts about his creative powers and fears of approaching senility. And in this same period one of fate's heaviest blows fell on him: the sudden break with Nadezhda Filaretovna von Meck. A passionate and highly romatic friendship of fourteen years was over. At her strange request, they had never met personally but had maintained a quite hearty and lovely correspondence (1200 letters had been exchanged, 764 of them by Tchaikovsky). She was a wealthy woman and had provided him much material support. He in turn had dedicated his Fourth Symphony to her. She had informed him of her decision to end their relations in a letter of September 1890 but had provided no explanation.

On the other hand this was also the time of greatest world recognition and triumphal glory for the composer. It was also the zenith of his now mature compositional abilities, for indeed, the ballet Nutcracker, the opera Iolanthe, and the Sixth Symphony lay yet before him. He was but fifty-one years of age and possessed much untapped vitality and interest in life, both of which are quite evident in his

*involvement in the upcoming trip to America. He was impatiently
awaiting news of the journey, when on January 15, 1891, Tchaikovsky received new details from Wolff. With his message, Wolff
enclosed a letter from the president of the New York Music Hall
Company, Morris Reno, which stated terms and specifications of
Tchaikovsky's participation in the festival. This news promptly proceeded from Tchaikovsky to Peter Ivanovich Jurgenson in Moscow.
Jurgenson, the founder and proprietor of the largest music publish-
ing house in Russia, was Tchaikovsky's publisher, trustee, crony,
and adviser in all his worldly affairs. Tchaikovsky liked him and
depended on him.*

PETER TCHAIKOVSKY TO PETER JURGENSON

Frolovskoe, January 15, 1891

My dear friend!

Wolff has sent me the letter from the American gentleman who arranged my invitation. It is so profitable and easily done that I would be mad to lose the chance of traveling
to America, a trip I have desired to make for so long. This
explains my telegram of yesterday. In America, when they
learned by cable that I suffered pains in my arm and would
not come, they became very anxious and now impatiently
await my answer: yes or no.

Please find out who is coming to visit me on Saturday
and Sunday and at what time.[3]

Answer immediately.

Yours,
P. Tchaikovsky

*At that time Tchaikovsky suffered from neuralgia of his right arm
and could not conduct. As a result, many of his concerts were can-
celled. Not wanting to miss the tour to America, he asked Jurgenson
to inform Hermann Wolff about it. In response Tchaikovsky received this letter from Jurgenson:*

Moscow, January 15, 1891

Dear friend,

I received your dispatch at 6:00 p.m. and in five minutes I sent one to Wolff: "Reise jedenfalls nach Amerika. Tchaikovsky." So you've adopted a decision! Good luck!

Jurgenson

Having accepted the invitation Tchaikovsky began his preparations for America.

PETER TCHAIKOVSKY TO PETER JURGENSON

Frolovskoe, January 17, 1891

Dear soul!

Send me at once my Legend for chorus and also the Liturgy and other sacred pieces (3 Cherubim's Songs) but not the Vesper Service. I must choose pieces for the American Music Festival. Do you have Ratter's edition of the Children Songs? For the Legend I need the German text.

In regard to Saturday and Sunday, please find out precisely who, who, and who are going to come and bring me on Saturday your selection of the best snacks from Lapin's. I have only a Russian wine from Christy's. For Zverev I must have champagne—be kind enough to buy me two bottles of Ai and for us about ten bottles of Russian champagne, to which we will add fruits—like in summer. For this I need pineapple, oranges, and mandarins.

But I'd best make a special list of the necessary items. I embrace you!

Yours,
P. Tchaikovsky

Please forgive me for loading you with this burden. If for some reason you can't leave on Saturday, send all the things with someone else, whom I will then gild.

But if you must be in Moscow at all costs, then be sure to come on Sunday. However, I've had no mail for three days. Probably there will be news about all this. Today I'll get it.

Relatives of the celebrated composer, primarily his older brother Nikolay (Kolia, Nikolasha), and younger brothers Ippolit, Modest, and Anatoly (Modia and Tolia—twins) had a persisting concern about all things that happened to Tchaikovsky. Modest lived in Petersburg and was especially close to Tchaikovsky. A playwright and librettist, he was the author of the librettos of Tchaikovsky's operas The Queen of Spades *and* Iolanthe. *The composer was also in particularly close and frequent correspondence with Anatoly, a lawyer and vice-governor of Tiflis. All of his relatives awaited news of this out-of-the-way and out-of-the-ordinary voyage. Tchaikovsky kept them aware of his undertaking. His was a large family of five brothers and one sister; as fate willed, one was marked with genius. Perhaps all his life the composer bore a sense of guilt before his siblings. This may explain why in his relations with them, as evidenced by his letters, Tchaikovsky somewhat moderated his successes and instinctively exaggerated his moral and physical sufferings. Nonetheless, he loved his siblings very much and sympathized with Anatoly, who was not very successful in his career.*

PETER TCHAIKOVSKY TO ANATOLY TCHAIKOVSKY

Frolovskoe, January 22, 1891

Tolia!

How deeply I was upset to learn that you were late for the train on my and Alexey's account. Please do forgive me! From the time you left nothing in particular has happened. But that frost, thank God, is over! Today it is one degree. Modest and Laroche are staying with me. Both went to Moscow for a day. Modest rode off to see Mme. Savin in his Symphony.[4] I completed *Hamlet* at last and sent it out. Now am occupied in revising and correcting the score to *Queen of Spades*. At week's end I go to Petersburg for final negotiations with the Directorate concerning the opera and the ballet. Because of all this I decided it would be more economical and prudent not to go abroad but to stay here for about two months and work hard. In April I will go to America. I have received detailed information about how and what I'll be doing there. The duties are not too great, the fee is good, and I really don't want to miss such an opportunity, which, perhaps, will never turn up again. Am looking forward to your news from Kamenka. What were they all like there?

Am sending pictures with this letter.

I kiss my dear Pania.

I will write to Kokodes one of these days. The more I delay it, the more that lucky man will get.[5]

P. Tchaikovsky

PETER TCHAIKOVSKY TO PETER JURGENSON

Petersburg, January 31, 1891

My dear friend!

I am frightfully glad about Brandukov's and Colonne's success. As to your summer negotiations with Pogozhev—I can't help you. I definitely don't remember what numbers were there. I have already told Osip Ivanovich about it.

Please pay off the Kiev photographer's bill.

Modest is not acquainted with Osten Saken.

I don't know any details about the trip to America except that I must only conduct three times: (a) a symphony or suite; (b) a piano concerto; (c) a chorus. All this will occur in New York in May and all this you have already heard from me, when you were last at my house in Frolovskoe. You yourself promised to obtain the actual details. In your letter before last you blame yourself for being drunk. I assure you, this is nothing to be ashamed of. In the first place, while you were drunk you were quite charming and amusing; secondly, I am certain that it is good for you to allow yourself a good sip from time to time. Indeed it happens so rarely!

The handling of *The Queen of Spades* has been abominable. As a result of Figner's intrigue—he doesn't want anyone to replace his wife—the opera was withdrawn from the repertory at the height of the season!!! And it received twelve sold-out performances at high prices![6]

I will be staying here longer than I thought, exactly a week and a half longer.

I embrace you.

P. T.

Almost simultaneously with the invitation to America, Tchaikovsky received a letter from Paris. His Parisian friend Felix Makkar, a music publisher and an active promoter of Tchaikovsky's music in France, asked him to conduct a concert of his compositions in Paris. The overture found a response.

PETER TCHAIKOVSKY TO FELIX MAKKAR

Frolovskoe, February 4, 1891

My dear friend,

I just received your kind letter! Regarding the proposed concert, we must first consider the following. I have been invited for the opening of a grand concert hall in New York. I must conduct three concerts and, in accordance with my promise, must arrive in New York on April 24. Thus I must depart from Le Havre not later than April 12. This means that the Parisian concert must take place not later than April 10.

Or, if you would prefer, I can return to Paris from New York. In that case I would not be in Paris rehearsing before May 25. It seems to me that this would be too late for our concert. In any case I would rather have it be before [the trip to] America for, who knows, I might stay on longer for the sake of a lucrative offer.

Consequently, before anything else, a concert hall of your choice must be reserved for April 7, 8, 9 or 10. As for the program, it should include a large symphony or suite (I'd prefer the Third, from which you know the variations), a symphonic poem *(Tempest, Francesca)* of your choice, then ballet pieces (something from *Voevoda* would be best—a work from my younger days which I revised and corrected this summer). Finally we should put singing and soloists in the program. I rely upon you.

That's all I can say for my part. As for an orchestra, I would prefer Colonne's, since I know it well—but again I give you full freedom in this matter.[7] Colonne will soon be in Moscow but I don't know whether I will see him. No one has come to me with a request to attend his concert.

In three days I go to Petersburg and will stay here until February 16 (French style). If you write me in Petersburg, the address is Moika, Hotel "Russia." Later I will return here.

A thousand greetings to Mme. Makkar and Mr. Noel.

All yours,
P. Tchaikovsky

PETER TCHAIKOVSKY TO ANATOLY TCHAIKOVSKY

Frolovskoe, February 12, 1891

Dear Tolia,

Have just returned from Petersburg where I spent two weeks and here found your letter. You ask about America. I've been invited to conduct three concerts which will take place in honor of the opening of a new concert hall in New York; at one of them I will conduct a symphony, at another, a piano concerto, at the third, several choruses. The first concert will be held on May 6 of the new style, but I promised to arrive ten days earlier. I should be there around April 12 of our style. I will depart from here around March 20. The honorarium they've offered me is certainly sufficient—$2500 (about 3000 roubles) and I go with the greatest pleasure, for I am very interested in the trip itself. I plan to return by June. It's quite likely that I will conduct a big concert in Paris before the American trip.

In Petersburg I conducted the Patriotic Concert with great success. At the theater they've done a terribly swinish thing to *Queen of Spades*. For no clear reason they stopped with the 12th performance, and have given no more. The alleged reason is that Figner won't sing with anyone but his wife. I haven't shown up at the theater since then and have received no explanation from anyone, but today I did write a letter to Vsevolozhsky in which I protest the injury done to me.[8] But to hell with them! Anyway as next year approaches I will agree to carry out their request that I write a ballet and a one-act opera, but only on the condition that I be officially protected from the whims of singers. On the whole I was thoroughly bored in Petersburg and am very glad to be back here again. My music for *Hamlet*, given for Gitry's benefit, pleased them all very much. Gitry was splendid. In a week I will go to Petersburg for a day to see Modest's play. Hope that your misunderstanding with Shervashidze can be settled. Be a little more patient. Have faith that you will succeed as you desire and the governorship will not escape you. But for the time being you can live quite pleasantly without the governorship in this world, especially in lovely Tiflis.

I fondly embrace you all.

Yours,
P. Tchaikovsky

PETER JURGENSON TO PETER TCHAIKOVSKY

Moscow, February 23, 1891

My dear friend,

Just now I received a letter from Tretbar.[9] You've been invited by Damrosch. He is the head of the Symphony Society and Assistant Conductor of the New York Opera. In

addition he is son-in-law to Minister Blaine, the American
de Giers.[10] The highest members of society (i.e., million-
aires) stand behind him, dutifully waiting until such time
that he deigns to request money from them. In May he will
be giving a *schickes* [stylish] *Musikfest*. The money is assured,
the orchestra is splendid, and you are guaranteed the finest, most exalted reception.

Tretbar, my friend and benefactor since 1876, asks that I
let him know without fail, on what ship you'll be traveling.
He is coming to meet you, even though by that time he will
be in his Tusculum, far from New York. They have already
received Wolff's telegram containing your consent.

Farewell!

Your
P. Jurgenson

The chest with the instruments was sent to you by mail
and today the receipt will be coming in a special envelope.

*In New York on the corner of Fifty-seventh Street and Seventh Av-
enue the massive edifice of the new Music Hall was now standing.
Interior work was coming to an end and preparations for the May
Festival could begin. The Oratorio Society and the Symphony Society
launched into a series of rehearsals to learn the many works selected
for the concert series. A myriad of practical and technical matters
had to be attended to. Soon the great event would arrive. On March
3, 1891, Morris Reno wrote a letter to Tchaikovsky:*

Dear Sir,

I had the pleasure of receiving your letter of February 6
and must tell you that all the gentlemen who took part in
our undertaking as well as the public itself have expressed
a most fervent desire that you participate in our Music Festival and now rejoice at this welcome event.

Perhaps it is unknown to you that both the late Dr. Leopold Damrosch, the founder of the Symphony Society, and

his son, Walter Damrosch, successor to him in the post of director for the above-named society, have performed your works with particular interest and success. Consequently Walter Damrosch, your faithful admirer, is overjoyed that you will be participating in our Gala Opening.

I have received both a cappella choruses that you so kindly sent to me and wish to thank you for them. I have added them to our program. Thus from among your works the program will include: two choruses, the Suite No. 3 in G Major and the Concerto in B-flat minor for piano and orchestra.

It is not necessary for you to bring the music; we already have the parts for both the Suite and the Concerto.

The opening of our Music Hall will take place on the evening of May 5 and will include the following: 1) Beethoven's Leonore Overture No. 3; 2) a special oratorio for the occasion; and 3) Berlioz' Te Deum.

I would be extremely pleased if, besides the listed works, we could hear performed on this same evening just after the oratorio a rather small work for orchestra written in a solemn character. It seems to me that your Solemn March would be perfectly suited to the event but if you prefer something else in that style I would be in complete agreement. In any case, whatever your choice (provided that it be a work by you, for orchestra, and in solemn character), please instruct your editor to send me by mail as soon as possible the score and all parts requested for a large orchestra. Of course I will pay the initial cost and all miscellaneous expenses.

I have just received Wolff's letter from Berlin in which he states that you are sending me through him a chorus chosen from among your older works. I suppose he means the Legend which you had already sent me together with the Pater Noster. In case it is something else, I will immediately inform you whether or not we can make use of it, taking into account that the time left to learn it is quite restricted.

I would be extremely indebted to you for prompt information on when you expect to arrive here and on what vessel. As I await the pleasure of meeting you, you may be assured, my dear sir, of my deepest respect.

Morris Reno

All the while musical life in New York was taking its normal course. The winter concert season of 1890–91 was at its height. Symphony concerts and open rehearsals occurred regularly in Irving Hall, Chickering Hall, Steinway Hall, and at the Metropolitan Opera. While Walter Damrosch directed the New York Symphony Society Orchestra, Theodore Thomas led the New York Philharmonic Society Orchestra, and the personal orchestras of Theodore Thomas and Anton Seidl also appeared in concert. Although works in the Germanic tradition still dominated the orchestral programs, the name Tchaikovsky came to appear more and more.

In his letter of February 2, 1891, Jurgenson reported to Tchaikovsky, "Tretbar writes that your Fifth Symphony was so well received in New York last year that Thomas was forced to reschedule it for a Philharmonic Society concert. Thomas asked me to inform you in the hope that it will give you pleasure." Another success followed soon after when Thomas premiered Tchaikovsky's Hamlet Fantasy Overture *with the Brooklyn Philharmonic on February 15, 1891. In the next day's* New York Evening Post *the eminent critic and musicologist Henry T. Fink described the concert:*

Evening Post, New York, February 16, 1891
Brooklyn Philharmonic

This Overture [Tchaikovsky's *Hamlet*] is one of the most important novelties produced here in many years, a composition which indicates that the gifted Russian composer, who is only fifty years old, is destined to become one of the greatest composers of this century. Indeed, his new "Hamlet" overture would establish his claim to that distinction had he written nothing else. It displays a marvellous mastery of all the technical details of composition and instrumentation—as wonderful in its way as the most brilliant feats of the greatest living pianists. But he does not, as Berlioz often does, use this technical skill to hide the absence of ideas. On the contrary, the "Hamlet" overture, which might be called a Symphonic Poem, teems with ideas, and is in this respect a worthy musical complement to Shakespeare's tragedy. And the music is so dramatically significant that it is not difficult to find in it the play after which it is named. We will call attention to only one striking detail. Musicians know what a weird, distant, super-terrestrial effect Wagner and other composers have produced by means of the tones of the "muted" French Horn. Now in Tchaikovsky's "Hamlet" there is a super-terrestrial horn note repeated slowly at least twenty times, while the other instruments weave ghostly harmonies around it. There can be no mistaking of this for anything but the apparition of Hamlet's father; and this touch, like many others, makes us long to hear some of Tchaikovsky's operas.

HENRY T. FINK TO PETER TCHAIKOVSKY

New York, February 19, 1891

Dear Sir,

I am a great admirer of your works and as a critic of the New York Evening Post I have frequently had the opportunity to analyze their merits. Your Hamlet Overture especially delighted me. I am enclosing my brief review of it, written after my first hearing. In certain places I ventured to infer a dramatic significance. Now I would be highly honored if you would inform me by letter (in English, French or German) whether my conjectures are correct or not.

Thank you in advance for your courtesy.

Your admirer,
Henry T. Fink

Two months later, after the second performance of the Hamlet
Overture in New York, Fink relayed the content of Tchaikovsky's
response to his readers:

Evening Post, New York, April 13, 1891

. . . To the Music-tired—and there are not a few towards
the close of a season—the most interesting piece on the
programme was of course the new and magnificent
Tchaikovsky overture ("Hamlet"). To a student of dramatic
music it is always an interesting task to guess what image or
idea was in the composer's mind when he wrote a certain
passage. Two months ago when the "Hamlet" overture was
played for the first time in this country, we wrote that the
oft-repeated muted horn note around which the other
instruments weave weird and ghostly harmonies undoubtedly
signifies the apparition of Hamlet's father. We have now
before us a letter from M. Tchaikovsky in which he says that
our conjecture was right: "L'explication que vous donnes de
l'episode ou le cor repete 12 fois note re en son bouche est
tout-a-fait juste." ["Your explanation of the episode where
the note "D" is repeated 12 times by the stopped French
Horn is perfectly correct."]

During the spring of 1891 the Boston Symphony under the direction
of Arthur Nikisch toured the major cities of several eastern and cen-
tral states. Tchaikovsky was represented with the following sym-
phonic works: Symphony No. 4, Romeo and Juliet, *and the Piano*
Concerto No. 1.[11]

Back at Frolovskoe Tchaikovsky's servant Sofronov had already
packed Tchaikovsky's bags in preparation for the long and arduous
journey which would take the composer to Moscow, Petersburg, Ber-
lin, Paris, Rouen, Le Havre, and, finally, New York. Tchaikovsky
left the village on March 2, 1891. Among the dearest ones Tchai-
kovsky left in Russia, his greatest affection was for his twenty-year-
old nephew Vladimir (Bob) Davidov, a son of the composer's younger
sister Alexandra (Sasha). He was a law student and lived in Peters-

burg with Tchaikovsky's older brother Nikolay (Kolia). While away Tchaikovsky wrote his first letter to his beloved nephew.

PETER TCHAIKOVSKY TO VLADIMIR DAVIDOV

Berlin, March 20, 1891

I've been aching to write you even though nothing interesting has happened as yet. At the start of my trip I felt pretty well and could read with enjoyment. But the next day I sensed the onset of that terrible, inexpressible, fiercely poignant despair which sometimes overcomes me when I am alone in strange lands. During such times one feels quite strongly his love for dear ones. Most of all I've thought—naturally—about you, yearned to see you, to hear your voice—this has become in my mind an unattainable bliss for which I would give ten years of my life (and you know I esteem life very much) if you could appear for only a second. For this kind of yearning, which you have probably never experienced and which is the most poignant in the world, I have only one remedy—drunkenness. And indeed I did drink an incredible amount of wine and cognac, between Eidkunnen and Berlin. As a result, I slept, though with difficulty. Arrived here this morning entirely surrounded by winter, i.e., found everything covered by a dense coat of snow and frozen. Today I am already less homesick, although a kind of leech still sticks to my heart. I feel weak, heavy in the head, and have decided to spend the night in Berlin. I've been to see Wolff (organizer of my American tour). Everything is arranged and settled. Visited Bock (a very dear man, my publisher from time to time). Assured everyone that I will leave tonight and now sit at home writing to you. Now I will go to dinner, take a long walk around the city and drop in on a concert where they are playing my 1812 Overture and the Andante from a quartet. Quite pleasant to listen to one's own works amidst a foreign audience and not be recognized by anyone. Tomorrow I depart. My next letter will be from Paris. Bob! I adore you. Remember how I told you that my joy at seeing you is less in comparison to the suffering when I am without you. Yet in strange lands, seeing before me the countless number of days, weeks, and months without you—I feel most strongly the full significance of my love for you. I embrace you!!

P. T.

I send this letter to the school so that Kolia will not read it.

PETER TCHAIKOVSKY TO ANATOLY TCHAIKOVSKY

Berlin, March 20, 1891

Golubchik Tolia!

Your letter was handed to me just as I boarded the train to go abroad. I read it with the liveliest interest. What a ball the general's wife gave! God, how I wish I'd been there!

This time I spent only three days in Petersburg. Saw all the relatives. All, thank God, are well and happy. I promised the Directorate to write a ballet and opera for the next season but warned them that, perhaps, my trip will not allow me to fulfill such a great task. Shall attempt to work at sea. Already on my way here I wrote a bit of the ballet. The main thing is to dispose of the ballet, but the opera so absorbs me and its subject is so pleasing to me that, give me two weeks of peace—and I may finish it on time. But we'll see. I was so tired from the trip that I decided to spend a night in Berlin. Tomorrow I go to Paris, which will be a pleasure, for Modest and Sapelnikov are there and I'll be glad to see them. On April 5 I will conduct a grand concert of my works there, again with Colonne's orchestra, which I directed three years before. I'll write you from Paris and America and request that you write me in New York at the following address: America. New York. P. Tchaikovsky, Steinway Hall. U.S.A. New York.

May God grant that your official matter be resolved, but I will be sad if you abandon Tiflis.

Can you imagine what a ninny this Katerina Ivanovna Sinelnikova-Laroche is! She is coming with me to America, i.e., on the same ship. Now I don't know if I should be pleased or distressed—more than likely I'll be glad for the presence of a familiar face. Tell Kokodes to wait a little bit for his subsidy. Extend the warmest embrace from me to Panichka and Tata, whose letter fascinated me.

I kiss you.

P. Tchaikovsky

PETER TCHAIKOVSKY TO PETER JURGENSON

Berlin, March 20, 1891

My dear soul!

Your message was handed to me at the moment I got in to ride to the train, therefore I am answering from Berlin. In my opinion it would be better to give the intermedia a French title: "Bergère fidèle" or "Fidélité de la Bergère." [The third scene of the opera *Queen of Spades*.] Let Sofia Ivanovna choose one of these titles.

If I am as wildly homesick as I was on the way here then I believe I'll never reach America but will flee home in shame half an hour before the ship leaves. I beg you, go-lubchik, write to me in Paris (up until April 3 of the new style), but more importantly—later—in New York. No doubt I will ache desperately for news from the homeland.

Have visited Wolff. They both, I mean he and his brother (who has traveled a good deal all over America) suggest that I take not a French but a German ship; for that I should first travel from Paris to Southampton. Wolff (the younger) now attempts to arrange all sorts of comforts and conveniences for me. He will send me the details in Paris. Have been to see Bock. He's grown terribly thin; says he was quite sick.

They've chased me out of Frolovskoe. Alexey will probably rent from Novikov. By the way, on April 1 I sent Alexey to collect 150 roubles from you (after Passover, perhaps 200) for I give out gifts of money to all my servants for the holidays. Please give him the money.

God bless you! Remember me to all.

Yours,
P. Tchaikovsky

Thoughts of Nadezhda Filaretovna von Meck had not left Tchaikovsky even for a day. He did not attempt to write her anymore but still hoped to maintain their friendship somehow—through his correspondence with the violinist and composer Vladislav Albertovich Pakhulsky, who was her son-in-law and secretary.

PETER TCHAIKOVSKY TO VLADISLAV PAKHULSKY

14 Rue Richepanse, Paris, March 25, 1891

Dear Vladislav Albertovich,

Your letter addressed to me in Moscow came to me today and I thank you for it. I never thought of complaining about your long silence, for I knew well what a pack of troubles have resulted from your trip and resettlement in Nice. I'm pleased that Nadezhda Filaretovna survived the trip and can assure you that the miraculous climate of Nice will soon completely restore her health.

Since I wrote you last time, great changes have taken place in my plans and intentions. I have accepted an invitation to go to New York to conduct at a great music festival in early May of the new style. Besides that, Colonne has invited me to conduct one concert here (on April 5) and so now I'm in Paris. Soon after the concert I will board the ship in Le Havre and set off for America.

I really don't know whether I should rejoice or lament this prospective trip. I agreed to it mainly so that I could recover from the many serious misfortunes which have befallen me during the last months of my life. Principles on which I've depended, believing them to be firm, give way one by one beneath me and I suddenly find myself on unstable ground. All has become odious to me. I need to escape to somewhere far away, to pull myself together. Meanwhile I am suffering at the hands of both Imperial Theaters. This winter in Moscow my operas were not given at all! In Petersburg *Queen of Spades* was taken from the repertory at the height of the season. All their rotten, offensive squabbles are so loathsome to think about!

Bow for me and greet Nadezhda Filaretovna and Julia Karlovna. I embrace you.

Sincerely yours,
P. Tchaikovsky

I am turned out of Frolovskoe!!! I know not where I'll live.

PETER TCHAIKOVSKY TO KONSTANTIN ROMANOV[12]

Paris, March 27, 1891

Your Imperial Highness!

The well-known Parisian conductor E. Colonne, who is now en route to Petersburg to conduct three concerts has asked me to provide him with letters of recommendation addressed to certain high-ranking personages.

Since among all high-ranking lovers of music you are my only personal acquaintance I have decided to send the letter of recommendation to you now which he will later bring before you. For God's sake please excuse my boldness. I concluded that if Colonne should call upon you while you were at home, then perhaps you would not be greatly inconvenienced in granting him two minutes of conversation—it would be for him both a great happiness and an inestimable honor.

During the course of last winter a series of unfavourable

circumstances gave me but rare opportunity to visit Your
Highness and the Grand Duchess, for which I am truly
sorry. My wish is ever to speak with you often and at
length. At the present time I am in Paris, where I am to
conduct a grand concert on April 5 (March 24), after which
I go to America, where I've been invited to participate as a
conductor in a Festival being held in New York on May 5
(April 23) upon the occasion of the opening of a new Music
Hall.

In the middle of June I hope to return to Russia.

I humbly beg Your Imperial Highness to extend my respectful greetings to the Grand Duchess.

Faithfully yours,
P. Tchaikovsky

PETER TCHAIKOVSKY TO PETER JURGENSON

Paris, March 29, 1891

For the last time, please send Mme. Alexandrova (Malaya
Nikitskaya, c/o Tsvetukhin) fifty roubles in silver. Don't be
cross. She is indeed troublesome, but still badly in need of
money.

It is settled that I am going by French steamer—have already bought the ticket and have a private cabin. After the
concert, which occurs on April 5 (March 24), I will probably go to Rouen the next day and work there for twelve
days. On April 18 (6) the steamer departs. If there is need
to write me about something urgent, address the letter
here, 14 Rue Richepanse—they will forward it to me in
Rouen. But if there is any change in my plans, I will let you
know. This is positively the last time in my life that I will
engage in such foolishness, i.e., mix and mingle with the
foreign public. It is difficult to express how much I suffer
in the depths of my soul and how deeply unhappy I am.
And what is it all for???

Yours,
P. Tchaikovsky

With this letter I enclose the letter of a Mr. Mirimanian from Tiflis. Answer him please. It concerns you.

My regards to all.

PETER TCHAIKOVSKY TO PETER JURGENSON

April 11, 1891, Rouen

I've fled here for a few days away from Parisian noise and anxiety; I am going to work at least a little, otherwise, I think, I will not be able to keep my promise. Am writing nothing about the concert for I hope you will learn of it from newspapers. I am so tired from all I've suffered in Paris that I make an oath to myself never again to accept such torture voluntarily. I would be delighted to refuse New York,—but this is impossible; I have even received a deposit already. Next Thursday Sapelnikov, Menter, and Modest will come here; they will see me off to Le Havre, where on Friday evening I will settle onto the ship to leave Le Havre at 5 a.m.

In answer to your questions:

1) The orchestra parts of *Hamlet* are definitely in your hands. The last time I performed *Hamlet* in December 1889 at Belyaev's, I brought parts and gave them to you along with the corrected score.

2) You ask why I printed the parts of the Legend in Hamburg. I didn't print them anywhere, but simply sent the score of the Legend (for chorus) with an added German text, two months ago. Ratter has had the parts printed at his own request. Why I was bothered with proofreading, I cannot understand. Oh, my dear, how deeply I regret that I have previously agreed to publish my things before performing. I find my Third Suite to be the most gratifying of all my orchestral pieces going abroad. Nevertheless it is necessary to modify it and publish in that form as I perform it, when it happens, that is, with various cuts and the altered orchestration. When will I get the chance to revise and make the second edition??? It's greatly desirable. It is published impeccably,—but I myself have made a lot of ter-

rible mistakes in it. The Second Concerto is impossible in
its present form too. I remember that you were about to
republish it,—but I don't know in what state the matter
stands. There are many very serious blunders on my part—
but there are countless errors in the parts too: no letters at
all—in a word, a shocking mess. I was worn out a good deal
at the rehearsals for this concerto. But am glad that the
new edition of the "Slavonic March" is so good. Every cloud
has a silver lining. When I feel that I am growing old and
am composed-out, I will occupy myself with bettering all
my things; and since I have bungled such a great deal in
my life—there will be plenty of work even if I live 90 years.

Address to New York so:

Hotel Normandie
Broadway 38th Street
U.S.A., New York

Rouen is interesting; I suffer boredom and despair but
am glad to be resting.

I embrace you.

P. Tchaikovsky

PETER TCHAIKOVSKY TO IVAN VSEVOLOZHSKY

Rouen, April 15, 1891

Dear Ivan Alexandrovich,

In accordance with my intention I have left Paris where I
spent three weeks and of course did not write a single
note—and gone to Rouen in order to work a little. And for
nearly a week I have actually worked during certain hours;
two days are left before the voyage to America. By that
time all outlines for the first two scenes of the ballet will be
ready. The question is, when will I finish all the rest? On
the way to America I will scarcely have the opportunity to
work. In the first place, my spirits are in an abominable
state owing to very intricate reasons upon which I shall not
elaborate in order not to tire you. Secondly, the impres-

sions of the sea, the bustle of a ship, no doubt some tossing about and above all the incessant tinkling on the piano by various English misses who will be my companions—all this will bother me. Thirdly, I am already disturbed by the emotions awaiting me in America. Thus it will be most prudent if I do not even attempt to work during the voyage. From the first day in America I must begin to rehearse the four concerts that I am obliged to conduct. Concerts will come next and along with them, banquets, receptions—in a word, various activities incompatible with composing. On the return trip perhaps I shall be calmer in spirit and can work a little—but in any case shall accomplish very little. I shall return to Russia in late May or, more likely, early June. Then, through expending an incredible amount of effort I will have to compose an entire act of the ballet and an entire opera—true, only a one-act opera, but large enough. And following that I must orchestrate it all in order that it be ready in time. In a word I must perform a daring musical feat. Most likely I shall succeed. But there's another matter. For some time the prospect of urgent, tiresome labor has begun to scare me. Here in Rouen I have had to make every effort of will to expend my last ounce of strength in order to work. As a result something colorless, dull, hasty, and bad comes of it. The realization that the matter is not proceeding well preys upon me, tortures me, bringing me to tears and afflictions; a painful anxiety constantly gnaws at my heart that it has been a long time since I have felt as unhappy as I do now. I do wish to keep my promise (for at our last meeting it seems I indeed gave my word to complete the appointed task on time) but at the same time I am deeply convinced that nothing good either for the theater or for me will come of my excessive pains. As usually happens with very nervous and sensitive people, possessed of unbalanced and broken natures—all that is causing me so much bother and worry has now reached monstrous proportions and become some kind of feverish nightmare, giving me no peace, day or night. "Confiturenbourg,"[13] *Casse-noisette, King René's Daughter*—these images do not cheer me or bring me inspiration, but frighten, horrify, and haunt me while awake and asleep, teasing me that I shall never dispense with them. Finally (for God's sake, don't laugh—I am quite serious) in these last three days I have become simply sick from despair, fear, and the worst depression. Tonight I have rashly decided that things cannot go on like this and that I must suffer you the injury of my broken promise. Dear Ivan Alexandrovich! I love you terribly much and cannot bear it when you are angry with me—but I assure you, I simply have no more strength. In the meantime I have decided that it would be better for me to inform you now, beforehand, that it is impossible for me to finish the opera and ballet for the next season, in order that you could have time to make arrangements for their replacement with something else.

In view of the above, is it not better to postpone *Casse-noisette* and *King René's Daughter* until the 1892–93 season? Working without haste I will do very well with both of them—I feel it. The second act of the ballet could be made marvelously effective—but it demands finely wrought work—and for that I have no time and, more importantly, neither the proper spirit nor the desire to work. I do not even mention *King René's Daughter;* This is the richest subject for music and so warms me and inspires me that I don't doubt in its success, if only the opera does not come about as a result of tension and haste.

So, allow me, for God's sake, instead of performing that feat as promised (which would either destroy me or come out badly) to present to you by next spring ballet and opera scores worthy of those expectations which you rest upon me. I will make the trip to America without worries, doubts, and fears, will return home calm and relieved of the many emotions experienced in Paris and America, and will begin to work, little by little, certain that I will produce two *chefs-d'oeuvres* (excuse my fatuity). I console myself with the following thought. When you wrote me an answer to my letter apropos of the suspension of *Queen of Spades* you mentioned that nothing was required for the next season except my ballet and opera. But at that time you didn't know that His Majesty would have wished for *Tsar Kandavl* and that *Mlada* would have been feasible for production. Now you have these two big costume pieces and perhaps this circumstance will help you to temper your displeasure towards me. I earnestly desire that you would understand my situation and without displeasure agree to postpone *Casse-noisette* and *King René's Daughter* until the 1892–93 season.

At any event I see no other way out of that extreme in which I find myself. Could my music for these two plots ever be good if I write it while bereft of strength and with despair at my heart, knowing full well that everything coming out would be bad, trite, vulgar, dull, and boring?

Now the thought that you are angry with me will torment me and prey upon me. In order for me to find out whether this is so or if, on the contrary, to my unimaginable joy, you have agreed to postpone the ballet and opera until after the coming season, I most earnestly beg you to write me a few words at the following address:

Mr. Tchaikovsky
Hotel Normandie
Broadway 38th Street
New York, U.S.A.

Faithfully yours,
P. Tchaikovsky

At that time Modest Tchaikovsky was also in France. On April 10 he came to Tchaikovsky in Rouen bringing tragic tidings, just received from Russia: their sister Alexandra Davidov had died after a long illness. But Modest could not bear to tell Peter. It would have been too painful a blow to the composer, who was about to leave on his transatlantic voyage. Therefore, Modest pleaded insurmountable homesickness and a desperate longing for relatives and left for Petersburg that very day.

PETER TCHAIKOVSKY TO MODEST TCHAIKOVSKY

Rouen, April 15, 1891

Dear Modia,

After your departure my agonies and tortures began and continued in crescendo until yesterday evening I reached a crisis which ended in my writing a long letter to I. A. Vsevolozhsky. Now a load is off my mind and I am recovered from three-days' madness. The main reason for my despair was that I had exerted myself to work in vain. Nothing came of it but mediocrity. Meanwhile *Casse-noisette* and *King René's Daughter* changed into horrifying, feverish nightmares which are beyond my powers of expression. I was simply tormented by the realization that I was completely incapable of effectively finishing the task I had accepted. And the prospect of constant tension on the way to America and in America and upon my return became a terrible, murderous phantom. It is difficult to convey everything that I have suffered but I don't remember ever being so unhappy. And as background to the tortures for me as composer, add to that my homesickness, which I had foreseen and which never deserts me when I am out of Russia. Finally I decided last night that this could not go on, and in the morning wrote a long letter to Vsevolozhsky, in which I ask that he not be angry with me for not presenting him with the opera and ballet earlier than for the 1892–93 season. Now a load is off my mind. Indeed why should I torture and strain myself? Can anything good result from such efforts? Now I've come to detest *King René's Daughter*. And the whole point is that I must love it!!! So in a word I must go to America absolved of this excessive, demanding toil or otherwise I will simply go mad. Even now I've been so nervous that as I wrote to Vsevolozhsky and write to you I feel a feverish, nervous shudder. No! To hell with the strain, urgency, and pangs of conscience. I still feel that I can create a *chef d'oeuvre* from *King René's Daughter* but not under these conditions.

The purpose of this letter is to induce you to go to Vsevolozhsky's and convince him not to be angry with me. If he doesn't understand the reasons for my resolution (they actually think I can sit down and write an opera in five minutes) explain to him that I'm not in a position to keep my promise, that I am very tired of these Parisian emotions, that I expect more of the same in America, etc., etc.

Today am going back to Paris to unwind. I have nothing to say about Rouen because I didn't see anything, except the art gallery, which I liked very much. The weather is the same—cold and dull. On the whole, Rouen is distasteful to me. I was in a theater, but not long (Musette).

You, lucky one, are already in Russia . . .

I embrace you, Bob, Kolia.

Ah, what a load is off my mind.

P. I. Tchaikovsky

PETER TCHAIKOVSKY TO MODEST TCHAIKOVSKY

Paris, April 16, 1891

Modia!

Yesterday, after sending you and Vsevolozhsky letters, I went to Paris. On the way to Menter's I dropped by the Cabinet de Lecture in the Passage de l'Opéra, well known to me. Picking up *Novoe Vremya* I saw on the last page that Sasha had died.[14] I ran out like I'd been stung. Reached Menter's and Vasia's only much later. What a blessing that they were here! I spent the night with them. Tonight I leave for Rouen and Le Havre. I first believed it was my duty to forget America and return to Petersburg but then I realized this would be fruitless. Besides I would have to return 5000 francs to New York that were received in advance and forfeit the balance and the ticket. No, I will go to America. My conscience pains me greatly. Am frightfully worried for Bob's sake even though I know by my own experience that at his age such griefs are taken indeed rather lightly. But I am especially sorry for Leva and Nata. These two must be suffering unbearably.

And so I go today to Rouen, tomorrow to Le Havre, and at 5 a.m., Saturday morning, will be at sea.

I cabled Kolia today—for God's sake send all details to New York immediately. Today more so than yesterday and the day before I am quite incapable of rendering "Confiturenbourg" in music.

I embrace all of you.

P. Tchaikovsky

I don't live in the Hotel Terminus at all but dropped by the cafe purely by chance.

PETER TCHAIKOVSKY TO ALEXEY SOFRONOV

April 17, 1891

Dear Lenia,

For a long time I have meant to write you but I have been working painstakingly and have had no time for letters. Today I go to Le Havre and tonight board the ship, which sails tomorrow at 5 a.m. As I leave I'm in a sad and sorry state! Yesterday, by chance, I read in the newspaper of Alexandra Ilyinichna's death. Oh, how gladly I would go home, but it can't be—I received a part of the money in advance and have already managed to spend it. However, nothing will make me stay in America for longer than two weeks—therefore, Lord willing, I will be back home by May 20. My health, thank God, is excellent. Concerning the move to Maidanovo, do as you wish. Perhaps before Passover you'll hear of something more suitable—then leave

Maidanovo. But, I repeat, do as you wish—just have everything settled for my arrival.

Stay well. I embrace you.

My regards to Katia, Petrovich, and Demyanovna.

Yours,
P. Tchaikovsky

PETER TCHAIKOVSKY TO MODEST TCHAIKOVSKY

April 18–27, 1891
Atlantic Ocean—New York   9 o'clock in the evening

I am going to write a diary of my passage and send it to
you upon my arrival in New York—and, please, save it, for
I mean to write an article based on this diary. I departed
Paris the day before yesterday. Vasia, Menter, and Conius
saw me off. Spent the night in odious Rouen, packed in the
morning and at 2 o'clock started for Le Havre. From the
rail station set off right to the dock and occupied my cabin.
The steamer is one of the most colossal and sumptuous
anywhere. Dined in town, gadded about, and at 10 o'clock
settled in my cabin. Till now the thought of the trip, the
bustle associated with the trip, my expectations of the
ocean—all this has given me considerable distraction. But
finding myself in my cabin, I felt more deeply unhappy
than ever before. The main reason is that I am annoyed
for not having received an answer to my telegram to Kolia
and still don't know why. No doubt it is a common tele-
graphic befuddlement—but it was terribly painful to leave
without news from Petersburg. Katerina Ivanovna was not
on the ship yesterday—I fervently desired that she had
been. Went to bed consoling myself with the thought that
she would come, as most passengers on the special train,
right at the hour of departure. Today, awaking late (at 8),
when the steamer was already going full speed, I left my
cabin convinced that I would find her among the passengers . . . but alas! She's not here. For a long time I let my-

self hope that she had slept late and would appear later. Oh, how wildly I long for this!!! No—truly—without exaggeration I say that I have never felt so miserable, lonely, and unhappy! The thought that I must sail yet another week, that only in New York will I have any news, horrifies me. Damn this trip!!!

The steamer is remarkably sumptuous—a true floating palace. There are not too many passengers—in first class only 80 people. Every day is the same. At 7 o'clock they serve tea or coffee which one can then ask to bring to the cabin. From 9 to 11, breakfast—i.e., after taking a seat, one may ask for as many dishes as he wants (the menu features about 10). You're free to eat when you want, only not earlier than 9 and not later than 11. At 1:30 comes lunch, i.e., yet another bountiful breakfast. I refused it, but was apparently the only one. Dinner at 5:30 is very plentiful and delicious. I sit at a rather small table with some American family. Very uncomfortable and boring.

At 5 o'clock we had a tragedy, which fell as heavily upon me as it did upon all the other passengers. I was down below, when suddenly a whistle sounded, the ship came to a halt, and the general commotion and uproar rose; in an instant they'd lowered a life-boat. Rushing up on deck I learned the following. A young man from second class had suddenly pulled his wallet out from his pocket, written several lines, jumped onto the railing, and thrown himself into the water. They threw down a lifebelt and the small boat immediately began its search. All of us looked on in silent terror. But nothing appeared on the surface and after half an hour the boat returned and we continued our course. In his wallet were found 35 francs and a barely decipherable note written on a little leaf from the notebook, saying (I myself read it and was even the first to understand the initial words, for the note was in German and all the passengers were American or French): "Ich bin unschuldig; der Bursche weiss . . ." ["I'm innocent; that fellow knows"], and then some scribbling which no one could make out. It's evident from the passengers' conversation that the young man had attracted attention all day long because of his eccentricities and that he was clearly insane.

After dinner I roamed around on deck. Soon my thirst for companionship became so strong that I went to the second class section and there located the *commis-voyageur* [Fr., commercial traveler] who yesterday rode with me from Rouen and was quite gay and talkative. Found him and chatted. But I feel no easier for it.

The weather is magnificent; the sea is calm and the ship is going so quietly and smoothly that one sometimes forgets that he is not on land. Just now we saw a lighthouse on the western end of England. That's the last bit of land until New York itself.

Under other traveling conditions, if certain things hadn't taken place, and if somebody (at least, e.g., Kat[erina] Iv[anovna]) were with me, then I could simply enjoy this trip.

And still I don't understand why Kolia didn't answer. When I left Rouen I ordered them to forward the text of the telegram to the dock. If it didn't come that means that two entire days have passed since my dispatch!!! The most improbable and terrible things are coming to my mind and I am especially anxious for Bob.

April 19
8 o'clock in the evening

In the morning the rocking began and gradually increased until it reached the point that I was overcome by inexpressible fright. But I am quite soothed by the fact that nearly all passengers who have sailed frequently are not in the least afraid of the thing that frightens me, i.e., destruction, but a few, a very few, are afraid of seasickness. The latter does not frighten me at all, for I don't feel the slightest trace of it. *Les garçons* with whom I've discussed the rocking say that it is merely "une mer un peu grosse"—but how would it be if it were tres grosse?!!!

The sight of the sea is beautiful and in those hours when

I am free of the fear, I enjoy the marvellous view. I am very interested in three huge sea-gulls (probably alba-trosses), which persistently follow us. I was told that they will go with us to Terre-Neuve. But when do they rest and how do they pass the night?

I read all day long, for except reading I can think of nothing to do. Composing disgusts me. A grief continues to gnaw at me. My fellow commis-voyageur, when I tried to pour out my feelings to him, said: "Et bien, à votre âge c'est assez naturel" ["At your age it is quite natural"], which hurt me very much. And yet he is the nicest and merriest fellow. I chatted with him and his pals several times today. The steward from the smoking lounge invited me to partic-ipate in a bet over how many miles we would travel before 12 o'clock. I gave the required 5 francs and at 12:15 he brought me 50. As it turned out, I'd won—how? I don't understand it.

At dinner I was obliged to converse with an unlikable French lady who sits opposite me. Seems there's one more week to sail. I'd better not say what I'm feeling. I only know that it is for the last time . . . No, at my age one must stay at home, close to his people. The thought that I am so distant from all close ones is simply killing me. Still, thank God, I am perfectly healthy.

Yesterday throughout the entire evening one miss sang Italian songs so cheekily and abominably that I was sur-prised no one made any rude comments to her.

April 20

Spent the night very well. When everyone had gone to bed, I walked for a long time on deck, in a coat (which serves as dressing gown) and slippers. The wind quieted down and when I descended to my cabin all was sufficiently calm. Today the weather is sunny but there is a wind, which began about midday and gradually increased. Now the ship rocks not side to side but forward to back but the vessel is so immense that comparatively few have been ill. Today I experienced a bit of anxiety, but then I also felt seasick at times. My friendship with the French commis-voyageur and his pals (all are in second class) grows ever closer. They are very lively and quick and I get along some-how much easier with them than with the sedate and sol-emn first class passengers. One of my new pals is the son of a rich ship-owner who's in the business of codfishing in Terre-Neuve. In a very curious French patois he related to me details of codfishing. They own several sailing vessels, which go out to sea (as Pierre Loti describes it) to fish for many months, and this young man (he is about 18) has made sea voyages of this kind several times already and managed to experience a great deal. At their invitation I went with them to the second class where they called for a poor emigrant who is traveling to America with his trained monkey. The latter performed various tricks for us. The state of my head and soul is most unusual. I'm getting used to not thinking about all the things that torment me, i.e., about home, Russia, and my people. I compel myself to think only about the ship, about how to consume time by reading, walking, talking with Frenchmen, eating,—and, most of all, by contemplating the sea, which is indescribably beautiful today in the sunlight. The sunset was astonishing. Thus within me I feel not my own self but someone else, who is sailing on the ocean and experiencing the interests of the moment. Sasha's death and all the tortures con-nected with my thoughts of her seem like reminiscences from a very remote past, which I, with no particular effort, try to banish so I can return to the present interests of that not-me—within me—who sails to America. The first class passengers that I encounter banal American men and women—very dandified, but not in the least congenial. Of more interest to me than my other first class companions is one Canadian bishop with his secretary. He had gone for the Pope's blessing. Yesterday he celebrated *une messe basse* [low mass] in a special cabin, which I dropped into by chance. The tossing is increasing as I am writing. But I now realize there can be no ocean without tossing and am adjusting to it. Now I go to bed.

April 21

In the night the tossing was so intense that I awoke, overcome with terror, a beating heart, and almost a fever. But a good shot of cognac soon had a calming effect. I put on my coat and came out on deck. The night was moonlit and marvelous. Having seen that everything was proceeding as usual, I realized that there was positively no cause for alarm. Had the ship been in danger, the crew would certainly have seemed anxious. The wonder of an ocean, when it is not stormy but still agitated and a full moon shines in the night—is beautiful beyond words. Afterwards I fell into a perfect sleep. By morning the roughness had begun to calm down and little by little changed into quiet ripples. We sailed into the Gulf Stream. One notices it, because all suddenly seems warm as summer. All day long the passengers enjoyed themselves. I should mention that we have several hundred emigrants, mostly from the Alsace, traveling with us. As soon as the weather becomes good, they give a ball— it's quite pleasant to watch their dancing to the sounds of the accordion. The emigrants show no sign of sadness on their faces. Six courtesans of the lowest sort are sailing with us, all engaged by a single gentleman, whose business it is and who accompanies them. One of them is quite pretty and all my second class pals avail themselves of her charms. They are a miserable, featherless scrawny sight. My chief pal (commis-voyageur) is successfully courting a second class passenger and has already started an affair with her. When they retire to his cabin, his pals watch over her little boy and mother him. Just now I was invited by this merry bunch into second class [quarters], where my commis-voyageur amused me and the rest of the audience with the singing of *grivoise* [bawdy] couplets and caricatures of the

French legal system. He performed all of this with such
genuine good humor that I laughed with all my heart. The
unattractive lady who is my neighbor at the dinner table
and with whom I must now reluctantly converse turned out
to be the wife of a musician in the Boston Orchestra. Consequently the conversation today was about music. She
talked to me about Boston concerts and the musical life of
the area—things of interest to a musician.

Today we encountered several sailing vessels, a large
whale which sent up a glorious fountain, and a *cachalot*
[sperm whale]. But I missed seeing them both.

April 22

I had imagined that I was invulnerable to seasickness. It
turns out I am vulnerable. By night the weather had gradually deteriorated. When I rose at 7 o'clock it had gotten so
bad and the sea was so heavy that I enjoyed the opportunity
of watching enormous ocean waves. But later it became
worse and worse until at 2 p.m. it was so dreadful that
every moment I expected destruction. Of course, destruction is out of the question. This is quite ordinary, nasty Atlantic weather. Not only the captain and his mates, but all
the stewards accept it as the simple and common run of
things. But for me, who judges the ocean like the Mediter-
ranean,—for me it is like Hell itself. Everything is cracking,
we are either falling into an abyss or rising up to the
clouds, it is impossible even to think of going on deck for
the wind will instantly blow you down . . . in a word, it is
nasty and frightful without precedent. A large number of
passengers are sick but some of them don't care a fig and
even play piano, cards, etc. At breakfast I had no appetite.
Afterward I felt sick and at dinner I couldn't look at food
without aversion. After soup I left . . . I was assured that
by evening I would be better, but it became worse . . .

There's been a great tragedy. My wallet with 460 francs
in gold was stolen from the drawer above my bed. I suspect

the steward who attends to me. Have reported it to M. Le Commissaire. A notice was posted. Still for me it was obviously a theft. Fortunately I have some other money with me.

I don't seem to feel nauseated and yet it's still bad. The tossing is ever increasing. No possibility of sleep. Cognac and coffee were my only meal today.

April 23

The night was abominable. We were tossed from side to side so much that it was hardly possible to sleep. I fell asleep many times and woke up with every strong jolt. In the morning things got better and through the day till 4 o'clock it was quite tolerable. And yet at breakfast I couldn't swallow a bite. Then a new calamity arrived. As we approached Bancs de Sables, near to Terre-Neuve, we entered into a zone of dense fog, which clearly is customary for this place. This is the most dreadful thing at sea, for a collision, even with a small sailing vessel,—is a wreck. Our speed has been reduced and every 30 seconds they sound the siren, an apparatus that emits an horrific roar, rather like the bellow of a gigantic tiger. It has a terrible effect on the nerves. However, at the moment I am writing the fog is beginning to thin and the siren is roaring less often. The passengers have learned who I am and now various people constantly come up to me and ask if I am so-and-so. Then begin the flattery, compliments, and conversation. My acquaintances have increased to a great number and now I can find no place to walk alone. Wherever I go, I meet an acquaintance, who right away begins talking and walking next to me. Besides that, they pester me to play. I refuse— but it seems I will have to play something on that horrible piano to put an end to it. My only thoughts are: when will it all be over and when will I be home at last? I've had no other thoughts today. I count upon, ponder over, and dream about the bliss of homecoming. The fog is vanishing but the tossing is starting up again . . . Of my lost wallet, not a word, not a whisper.

> April 24
> 8 in the evening

Am absolutely in no position to write. Since yesterday evening I suffer terribly. A most vicious hurricane is blowing. Some say it was forecast by the meteorological observatory. It is indeed something horrible! But then it is more horrible for me, a novice. Many passengers don't care a fig. Some say that it will last till New York. My suffering is more emotional than physical. To put it bluntly—I am afraid and horrified.

> April 25
> 8 in the evening

After writing the above lines, I ascended to the *fumoir,* where usually in the evening there are many passengers— smoking, drinking, playing cards, dominoes, etc. Tonight only a few and all were sitting there thoughtfully and anxiously. I drank some punch and descended to my place. The hurricane grew yet worse. Lying down is out of the question. I sat in a corner of a little sofa and tried not to think about the goings-on—but is it possible not to think, when the noise, cracking, convulsive lurches of the whole ship and desperate wailing of the blast can't be stifled with anything?

I sat in such a state for a very long time; what went on in my soul is difficult to convey. Such a foul thing. Then I began to notice that bit by bit the tempest was calming down; that those dreadful jolts, when the screw comes out of the water and the shaking is unusually frightening,—were becoming less frequent; that the fury of the blast had become less violent . . . Then I fell asleep in the same pose, between my trunk and the wall of the cabin. Woke up at 5 a.m., when the tempest had already blown over. I fell sweetly back asleep. In the morning found out that we had been in the center of an unusually ferocious hurricane, of a sort that rarely occurs. At 10 p.m. it had been especially fierce. Today the weather continued to get better, beginning in the morning—and by 12 o'clock had turned quite pleasant. At 2 o'clock we encountered the long-awaited pilot. All the passengers poured out to look at him, as he waited for us in his tiny boat. The ship pulled to a halt and we took him on board. There are only about 24 hours left. In consequence of the storm we will be several hours late. I am very glad that the passage is coming to an end at last. Further stay on the ship would be unbearable for me. The main reason is that everyone now knows me, all want to start conversation, and there is no place except my cabin where I can be alone. Besides that, they pester me to play things and always start talking music. Lord! When will this all be over? I've decided to leave New York by German ship on April 30/May 12. Lord willing, about May 10 or soon after I will be back in Petersburg!!!!!!

New York
April 27

The rest of the trip was completed quite safely. The closer I came to New York, the more I became worried, lonely, dismayed, and above all, regretful, about this mad trip. Possibly, when everything ends happily I may remember it with interest, but now it is nothing but suffering.

Before New York there were endless formalities with the ship's arrival and customs. They require a full interrogation. Finally at 5:30 we landed. I was welcomed by four very courteous gentlemen and one lady and was at once driven to the hotel. Here I informed Mr. Morris Reno that I wanted to leave on the 12th. He responded that it would be impossible for an extraordinary concert had been announced for the 18th of which Wolff had said nothing. When all the gentlemen left I began to pace around the

rooms (there are two) and let fall many tears. I'd asked that
they let me have the entire evening free and therefore declined all dinner and evening invitations. After taking a
bath (bath, lavatory, and washbasin with hot and cold water
are in every room of the hotel) and changing, I dined
downstairs with aversion and went for a stroll on Broadway. A strange street! One- and two-story houses alternate
with nine-story buildings. Very original!!! After returning
home, I wept again. As is usual after tearful fits, the old
weeper fell dead asleep and woke up refreshed, but with a
new supply of tears ready to pour from my eyes.

Thank you for the telegram—it brought great consolation to me. Modia, let whomever you want read this letter
and then send it to Tolia, that he can return it to me. Who
knows, probably I will write an article after all.

I embrace you all.

P. Tchaikovsky

Am sending a clipping from today's *New York Herald.*

11

Twenty-five Days in America

Thus, one calm April evening, Tchaikovsky set foot on American soil. He had come from the other end of the earth—an alien with a burden of painful worries. He had not a single friend in America waiting to comfort him. But America was prepared to honor a celebrity and welcomed Tchaikovsky as a superstar, one of the greatest composers of the century. The press lavished attention on him: the New York Herald, Evening Post, Musical Courier, New York Morning Journal, New York World, New York Times, New York Tribune, Sun, Brooklyn Daily Eagle, Mail and Express, Press, Evening Telegram, Baltimore American, Baltimore Sun, Philadelphia Press, Philadelphia North American, *and the* Philadelphia Daily Evening Telegraph. *In the articles from these papers and journals, we find a fascinating mixture of talent, originality, and professionalism along with naïveté and amateurism. Some of the writers and observers deserve special praise for the high quality of their coverage of this remarkable event, in particular, the* New York Herald *(the name of the very sensitive and sympathetic correspondent is lost to oblivion). Modest Tchaikovsky acknowledged that the interview with Tchaikovsky on May 17, 1891, "is reproduced with astonishing fidelity. As we read it, we can almost imagine we can hear the voice of Tchaikovsky himself." The meticulously professional and erudite Henry Fink represented the* Evening Post;

sparkling, profound, and somewhat eccentric Marc A. Blumenberg, the weekly magazine, Musical Courier; *and the inventive soul Ivy Ross, the* New York Morning Journal.

Tchaikovsky stayed in America for twenty-five days. At the conclusion of his engagement at the Music Hall, he went to view the world's wonder, Niagara Falls; he visited Washington, D.C.; and he gave two concerts, one in Baltimore and one in Philadelphia. A wealth of written material was saved for posterity, and it depicts Tchaikovsky's journey to America day by day.

DAY FIRST

New York Times, April 26, 1891
Musical topics

Tchaikovsky, the famous Russian composer, who is to conduct some of his own compositions at the coming Music Festival at the Music Hall is expected to arrive here to-day by the steamer La Bretagne.

DIARY   April 26

When at last the endless landing procedure was over and I could leave the ship, Mr. and Mrs. Reno, Hyde,[15] Mayer (Knabe's representative[16]), Reno's daughter, and a young man came up to me. They quickly helped me to fulfill all the formalities of customs, seated me in a carriage next to lovely Miss Alice, and drove me to the Hotel Normandie. On the way I engaged in surprisingly courteous and surprisingly breezy (as if I rejoiced at all the goings-on) conversation with my companions. But in my heart there were a despair and desire to run miles and miles away. And yet in truth I must say that all these nice people accorded me the most cordial welcome. At the hotel a very comfortable suite (with lavatory and bath) was waiting for me, and

after the departure of my greeters, I settled myself therein.
Before anything else I had myself a good cry. Then I took
a bath, changed, and went to the restaurant downstairs. I
was put in the service of a French waiter, a very gentle man
(quite a comfort to me) but perhaps a bit daft. I dined
without any enjoyment. Went out on the street (a main
one: Broadway) and wandered about it a good while. Since
it was Sunday, the street was not especially animated. An
abundance of Negro faces startled me. After returning
home began to whimper several times again. Slept perfectly.

DAY SECOND

New York Daily Tribune, April 27, 1891
Arrival of a well-known composer

P. Tchaikovsky, a well-known composer, landed here yesterday from the steamship La Bretagne. He has come over to
join the Music Hall Company of New York, and will conduct
some of his own compositions in the Music Hall founded by
Andrew Carnegie at Fifty-seventh street and Seventh avenue.

Mr. Tchaikovsky, who was accompanied by his wife,[17] was
met at the dock by Morris Reno, who took him immediately
to the Hotel Normandie.

New York Herald, April 27, 1891
Tchaikovsky is here

The great Russian composer Peter Tchaikovsky arrived on
the French steamer La Bretagne yesterday and immediately
upon seeing to a few small pieces of luggage was driven to
his hotel.

The traveler carries his years well and, but for the white

in his beard and hair, looks every whit ten years younger than his biographers rate him.

He comes to take an active part in the May Festival, to be held in the new Carnegie Hall during the first week in May, when he will conduct a number of his own compositions.

As a composer Tchaikovsky holds a position in Russia equal, if not superior to that of Rubinstein himself, although the latter has a wider European reputation as a pianist.[18]

"I was seventeen years of age," said the composer, "when I made the acquaintance of my singing master, Piccioli, and his influence over me was enormous. Up to this day I hear the melodies of Bellini with tears in my eyes."

As with many others who rank high in his profession, Tchaikovsky began his youngmanhood as a lawyer's clerk, and not until he had passed his majority was he allowed to enter the conservatorium founded by Rubinstein.

In 1865 he was appointed Professor of Composition in the Moscow Conservatoire and served there until his illness in 1877, which compelled him to resign. Since then he has lived exclusively devoted to composition.

New York Times, April 27, 1891
The Music Hall managers and ticket speculators

To the editor of the *New York Times:*
In response to a communication in The Times this morning signed "Music," in which complaint is made about the presence of ticket speculators at the Music Hall when the sale of ticket for single performances was opened, I would state that official announcement was made by advertisement that "the sale of subscription tickets will begin at the box office of the Music Hall on Monday Morning, April 6, and will close Saturday, April 18"; also that "the sale for the single performances of the festival will begin Tuesday morning, April 21, at 9 o'clock, and continue daily until 6 p.m."

During the subscription sale instructions were given that

not more than six tickets should be sold to any one person and none to any known ticket speculator, and the officer stationed in the lobby could devise no scheme to prevent speculators from buying through third parties and duplicating their purchases through confederates. The sale of subscription tickets was closed seven days earlier than at first advertised, because it was found necessary to retain something for the purchasers of seats for single performances.

In the light of this information it is superfluous to say that the best situated seats could not be found by "Music" in the box office, where, however, he did not even to try to get seats. I will add that there is not a seat in the new Music Hall that does not command full view of the stage or is in any respect undesirable.

"Music's" information that the management of the Music Hall is in league with the speculators needs no denial with those who know us. There is no way of mitigating or stopping the nuisance so long, as these men are licensed by the city to pursue their unwelcome calling in front of our premises. If "Music" can suggest through the public any practical way by which we can rid ourselves of this trouble we will gladly adapt it.

Morris Reno
President of the Music Hall Company
of New York, N.Y., Friday, April 24, 1891

PETER TCHAIKOVSKY TO ANATOLY AND PANIA TCHAIKOVSKY

April 27, New York

Golubchiki Tolia and Pania,

Yesterday I arrived in New York. The sailing was safe but we did have a severe storm. While traveling I felt extremely sensitive and had an awful yearning in my soul. I kept a detailed diary and have sent it to Modest in order that he would read it himself, give it to all who want among close ones in Petersburg and then send to you. Despite the disgusting state of my spirits I feel entirely well. Now all my thoughts are directed toward escaping [from America] as soon as possible and going home. By the time this letter reaches you, I probably will be on the way to Russia. They greeted me here with honor and cordiality; today in all the newspapers there is already information on my arrival together with my portrait. It turns out that I am far better known in America than in Europe. Here I am a big shot.

New York is a very handsome and very original city. On the main street small one-story houses alternate with nine-story buildings. All has turned green, indeed there is much green—a joy for the eyes. I've not visited anybody yet and not seen anyone, but four very bland, courteous gentlemen and one lady welcomed me. I recall that at this very time two years ago I went from Marseilles to Batumi, and soon I am weeping. I've become a terrible crybaby in general. And yet all these are trifles; later I will recall this time with pleasure. So, from my diary you will know details of my trip. But for the present time I embrace and kiss you hard. I fondly kiss Tata. My regards and embraces to Kokodes.

DIARY   April 27

I wrote two letters[19] in my room upstairs and began expecting guests. Mayer came first. The sincere friendliness of this nice German surprises and touches me. Being the representative of a piano factory, he has not the least interest in wooing a musician if he is not a pianist. Right after him came a reporter with whom I could converse only because Mayer was here. Some of his questions were very curious. Then Reno and another very nice and affable gentleman appeared. Reno said to me that I was expected at the rehearsal. Sending the reporter on his way, we walked to the Music Hall (Reno, Mayer, and I). The building is magnificent. At the rehearsal they were finishing the finale of Beethoven's Fifth Symphony. I found Damrosch (conducting without a frock-coat) very likable. Upon finishing the symphony I headed straight for Damrosch, but had to stop at once to respond to the loud welcome of the orchestra. Damrosch delivered a brief speech. Ovation again. I could rehearse only the first and second movements of the suite. The orchestra is splendid. After the rehearsal Mayer and I went to breakfast, and after breakfast he led me around Broadway, helped me buy a hat, presented me with a hundred cigarettes, showed me the very interesting Hoffman Bar (decorated with splendid paintings, statues, and tapestries), and finally walked me home. Unbelievably tired, I lay down to sleep. Upon awaking, I began to dress in expectation of Reno, who appeared without delay. I tried to persuade him to release me from Philadelphia and Baltimore. He, I believe, has nothing against carrying out my request. We set out to his place on the Hoch-Bahn. His wife and daughters are very lovely and amiable. He led me to Damrosch as well. One year ago Damrosch married the daughter of a very rich and solemn man. We three dined together; both hosts are very attractive. With Damrosch to Mr. Hyde and to Mr. Carnegie. I like the latter,—a rich, old man possessing 30 million dollars who resembles Ostrovsky[20]—mainly because he adores Moscow, which he visited two years ago. No less than Moscow he loves Scottish songs, a considerable number of which Damrosch played for him on an excellent Steinway. His wife is young and quite nice. After these two visitations I also went along with Hyde and Damrosch to the Athletic Club and to another, more serious club, resembling our English Club. The Athletic Club astounded me, particularly the pool, where the members were swimming, and the upper gallery, where in winter they skate. At the serious club we had some soft drinks. Finally at 11 o'clock I was driven home. It is unnecessary to say that I was completely exhausted.

DAY THIRD

New York World, April 28, 1891
Russian great composer P. Tchaikovsky spends his first day
in New York

Gospodin Peter Ilyich Tchaikovsky, the Great Russian Composer, who was invited to visit the United States by Andrew
Carnegie, spent the first day in New York principally outside
of the Hotel Normandie. He was taken in charge by Messrs.
Walter Damrosch and Morris Reno, and one of his first visitors was the Pittsburgh iron master. Mr. Tchaikovsky spent
the first evening listening to the rehearsals at the Carnegie
Hall, now going on under the direction of Mr. Damrosch.
He intends to spend a year in America and his time will be
occupied at the series of concerts now being arranged for
him at which nearly all his great orchestral works will be produced. Tomorrow he will rehearse his "Marche Solonelle,"
his Suite No. 3, and afterwards his Concerto No. 1, all of
which together with some "a Cappella" numbers and songs
he will conduct at the coming Festival. He is desirous, however, that his Fifth Symphony shall be heard in New York,
and it is probable that some important changes may be made
in Mr. Damrosch's programme.

DIARY   April 28

Slept very well. Reinhard, the representative of Mayer-
Knabe came to visit me for the sole purpose of finding out
whether or not I needed anything! Astonishing people,
these Americans! Unlike the common impression of Paris,
where at each favor, at each grace from a stranger, one
senses an attempt at exploitation, American straightfor-
wardness, sincerity, generosity, cordiality without any ulte-
rior motive, readiness to serve you and coddle—it is all simply astounding and touching. These traits, along with
American customs, lifestyle, and habits in general are very

appealing to me—but I relish these things like a man who sits at a table of gastronomical marvels, but is bereft of appetite. My appetite can be restored only by the prospect of returning to Russia.

At 11 o'clock went roaming! I had breakfast in some rather fine restaurant. Came home at 1 o'clock and dozed. Reinhard (very likable young man) came so that we could go together to Mayer. We dropped in at the splendid Hoffman Bar. Knabe's store. Mayer led me to a photographer. Taking the elevator to about the ninth floor, we were received by a little old man in a red cap, who turned out to be the owner of the studio. I believe I have never seen a more original crackpot. This living parody of Napoleon III (closely resembling the original but in the sense of a caricature) at first twisted me in search of the good side of my face. Then for a long time he expanded upon the theory of the good side and performed experiments of this sort on Mayer as well. Next I was photographed in various poses. During the intermissions between posings, the old man amused me with some almost clownish antics. For all of his peculiarities, he is unusually appealing and cordial—again, in the American way. From there set out with Mayer in a carriage for the park. The park is new but nevertheless superb. A host of elegant carriages and ladies. Drove to pick up Mayer's wife and daughter, and continued the ride along the high bank of the Hudson. It began to get cold. The conversation with kind German-American ladies made me tired. Finally we drew up to the famous Delmonico restaurant. Here Mayer treated me to a luxurious dinner. He and his ladies drove me home. Changing into a tail-coat, I waited for Mr. Hyde. With him, his wife, Damrosch, the Renos, and young Thomas,[21] sat through an unusually boring concert at the big operatic theater. An orchestra and chorus of 500 people performed an oratorio, "Captivity," by the American composer Max Vogrich.[22] I have never before heard such banal and dull music. What an awful bore. I wanted to go home, but the ever-kind Hydes dragged me

with young Thomas to Delmonico's for supper. We ate oys-
ters, a sauce made of small turtles (!!!) and cheese. Champagne and some mint liquid sustained my fading spirits.
They drove me home at 12 o'clock. Telegram from Botkin,[23] calling me to Washington.

DAY FOURTH

DIARY   April 29

    Spent a restless night. After tea wrote letters.[24] Took a
walk on Fifth Avenue. What mansions it has! Had breakfast
at home alone. Mayer's place. The kindliness and attention
of this nice man simply astound me, but, out of my Parisian
habit, I still try to find out—just what does he want from
me? But no!—nothing. In the morning he sent Reinhard to
find out whether or not I needed anything, and indeed I
did require his help, for without him I would not have
known how to send a telegram to Washington. Came home
at 3 o'clock to await Mr. William von Sachs, a very amiable
and refined gentleman, a music lover, and writer on music.
While he was still here, my French traveling-pals May and
Buso appeared, along with a pal of theirs. I was very glad
and went to drink absinthe with them. Upon returning,
slept. At 7 o'clock Hyde and his wife came for me. What a
pity that I lack the words and shadings to describe these
two originals, who are so soft and kind to me. Of particular
interest is the language we must use to converse: it consists
of a most curious combination of English, French, and German words. Each word pronounced by Hyde in speaking to
me is the result of an enormous mental effort and sometimes an entire minute actually goes by until, from out of a
vague muttering, some highly unlikely word, foreign to all
three languages is finally uttered. Through it all Hyde
maintained his serious but kindly mien. They drove me to
the Renos', who gave a big dinner for my sake. Ladies came

dressed in evening gowns. The table was covered with flowers. Beside every lady's setting lay a bouquet and for men
there were little bunches of lilies of the valley, that the
men, upon sitting down, placed into holders on their coats.
Beside every lady's place stood a little portrait of me in a
delicate frame. The dinner began at 7:30 o'clock and ended
precisely at 11. I am writing this without the least exaggeration—such is the native tradition. It is impossible to enu-
merate all the dishes. In the middle of dinner they served
ice cream in little boxes to which were attached little writing
slates, pencils, and sponges. Written on the slates were excerpts from my works. Next I was asked to sign my autograph on the little slates. The conversation was very animated. I sat between Mrs. Reno and Mrs. Damrosch, a very
attractive and graceful lady. Opposite me the little old man
Carnegie had deigned to seat himself—Carnegie, venerator
of Moscow and possessor of 40 million dollars. His resemblance to Ostrovsky is striking. All the time he kept saying
that our church chorus must be brought to New York. At
11 o'clock, tormented by the need to smoke and driven to
nausea by the endless eating, I ventured to ask Mrs. Reno
if I could rise. Half an hour later all had departed.

DAY FIFTH

DIARY   April 30

   It's getting hard to write—I don't find the time. Had
breakfast with my French friends at their place, the Hotel
Mortm. Rendezvous with von Sachs near the post office.
We walked along the Brooklyn Bridge. From there we
headed for Schirmer's, the owner of the most spacious music store in America; and yet the store and especially the
metallography are quite inferior to Jurgenson's. Schirmer
asked to publish my works. At home I received the reporter Ivy Ross, who came to ask me to write a piece for

her paper, next the pianist Wilson, who thoroughly annoyed me. After her departure I sat on the sofa like a stone image for about an hour and a half, indulging in the pleasures of rest and solitude. I had no dinner. At 8:30 o'clock I was already at the Music Hall for the chorus rehearsal. The chorus greeted me with an ovation. They sang very well. On my departure from there I met near the exit the amiable architect who built the hall: he introduced me to a pleasant, rather full-bellied man, his chief assistant, whose talent and efficiency he couldn't praise enough. This man turned out to be a pure-blooded Russian, who had changed himself into an American citizen. The architect explained to me that he was an anarchist and a socialist. We talked Russian for some time with this countryman of mine and I promised to call on him. An interesting acquaintance. Just then I met the lovely Reno family. Devoted the rest of the evening to a light supper and stroll. Read and reread received letters. Wept as usual.

PETER TCHAIKOVSKY TO VLADIMIR DAVIDOV

April 30, 1891

Just received letters from Modia, Annette, and Jurgenson. It is impossible to express how precious letters are for one in my state. I was infinitely glad. From day to day I keep a detailed diary and on my return will give it to all of you to read—therefore, I will not go into particulars. All in all, New York, American customs, American hospitality, the very sight of the city, and the unusual comforts of the surroundings—all this is quite to my liking, and if I were younger, I would probably derive great pleasure from staying in this interesting, youthful country. But I bear all this as if it were an easy punishment, softened by favorable circumstances. Thought and aspiration are one: homeward, homeward, homeward!!! There is some hope that I will leave on the 12th. Everyone here pampers, honors, and entertains me. It turns out that I am ten times better known

in America then in Europe. At first, when they told me
that, I thought that it was an exaggerated compliment, but
now I see that it is the truth. Works of mine that are still
unknown in Moscow, are performed here several times a
season, and whole reviews and commentaries are written on
them (e.g., *Hamlet*). I am far more a big shot here than in
Russia. Is is not curious!!! I was enthusiastically received by
musicians at the rehearsal (till now there has been only
one). But you will learn all the precise details from my diary. Now I'll say a few words about New York itself. This is
a vast city, more strange and original than handsome.
There are long one-story houses, 11-story buildings, and
one building (a brand-new hotel) that is 17 stories high. But
in Chicago they went even further. There is a 21-story
building there!!! As for New York, this phenomenon can
be simply explained. The city is situated on a narrow
peninsula, surrounded by water on three sides, and can't
grow any wider; therefore, it grows up. They say that in 10
years all the buildings will reach at least 10 floors. But for
you the most interesting convention in New York is this:
every little apartment, every hotel accommodation has a
lavatory with a basin, bath, and washstand installed with hot
and cold running water. Splashing in the bath in the morning I always think of you. Lighting is by electricity and gas.
Candles are not used at all. In case of need, one acts differently than in Europe—namely, one rings and then says
what is required through a tube, with one's mouth by the
bell. Vice versa, if someone asks for me downstairs, they
ring and then report through the tube who came or what
they asked about. This is uncomfortable in view of my lack
of English. No one except servants ever walks upstairs. The
elevator runs constantly, going up and down at an incredible speed, to let the hotel's inhabitants and visitors in and
out. As for the streets, but for the novelty that little houses
alternate with huge buildings,—except for that peculiarity,
the street itself is neither especially noisy nor especially
crowded. The explanation is that there are hardly any cab-

bies or fiacres here. The traffic goes either by horsecars or on an actual railroad, with branches stretching over the whole vast city. Besides, in the morning, the entire population rushes to the East where "Downtown" is located, i.e., the part of the city with merchants' offices. In the evening all of them return home. They live as in London; every apartment is a separate house with several stories, in a word, extending vertically, not laterally. That's enough for the time being. Soon I will write again to one of you. I embrace you, my dear one, also Modest and Kolia.

How soon, how soon?

Yours,
P. Tchaikovsky

DAY SIXTH

DIARY   May 1

Rose late. Sat down to write an article for Miss Ivy. Reno appeared with the tidings that he'd already arranged a cabin for me on *Fürst Bismarck,* departing on 21st. God! How distant it still is!!! Called on the ever-kind Mayer with whom I had breakfast at an excellent Italian restaurant. We headed to Downtown on the elevated. Only then did I see what animation can develop on Broadway at some hours. Until now I'd judged the street by the parts that are nearest to the hotel, and they are not at all active. But this is the insignificant part of a street that is seven miles long. The buildings of Downtown are senselessly colossal; at least I fail to understand how one can live on the 13th floor. Mayer and I ascended to the roof of one such building; the sight from there was spectacular,—but my head swam when I looked down on the Broadway pavement. Then Mayer obtained permission for me to look at the government treasury with all its vaults, where hundreds of millions in gold,

silver, and new bills and banknotes are kept. Unusually polite, but still important officials led us through these vaults,
opening monumental doors with mysterious locks by the
equally mysterious turning of some metal knobs. Sacks of
gold, resembling sacks of flour in storehouses, repose in
cute, neat little storerooms, lighted by electricity. They allowed me to hold a bundle of new bills for a while, which
were valued at $10,000,000. At last I understood why gold
and silver are not in circulation; only here did this oddity
become clear to me. It turns out that an American prefers
filthy, detestable pieces of paper to metal, finding them
more convenient and practical. But then these pieces of paper—odd as it may seem to us—are valued more than gold
and silver, thanks to the immense supply of precious metals
kept in the treasury. From the treasury we started for the
ever-kind Mr. Hyde's place of business. He is a director of
some banking establishment as well and thus could also
lead me through vaults, showing me mountains of bills kept
there. We were also at the Stock Exchange, which seemed
to me somewhat quieter than the Parisian one. Hyde
treated us to a lemonade in a local cafe. Finally we headed
for home, again via the elevated.

During this interesting tour I felt a certain, probably se-
nile, abominable fatigue. Reaching home, I had still to complete the article (on Wagner) for Miss Ivy. And at 5 o'clock
I was already hurrying to Mr. William von Sachs. He lives
in a vast building, in which only unmarried men can rent
suites. Women are admitted in this strange American mon-
astery only as guests. The building itself and Sachs's apartment are very elegant and refined. I found there a little
company, which gradually increased until we amounted to
a fair number. We were to have 5 o'clock tea. The pianist
Wilson played (visited me yesterday), a great admirer of
Russian music. She played, by the way, a marvelous serenade by Borodin. Having disposed of invitations, I spent
the evening alone. God, how pleasant it was! I dined in
Hoffman's Restaurant, as usual without any enjoyment.

Walking far up Broadway, I stumbled upon a meeting of socialists wearing red caps. As I learned from newspapers on following days, there were 5000 people with banners, huge lanterns, and inscriptions on them like the following: "Brothers! We are slaves in free America! We don't want to work more than 8 hours!" However, to me this demonstration seemed to be nothing but buffoonery; and natives, I believe, feel the same way, judging that there were few curious ones and the public circulated entirely as every day. Went to sleep physically tired but somehow emotionally relaxed.

DAY SEVENTH

Mail and Express, May 2, 1891
The festival at the new Music Hall next week

Peter Ilyich Tchaikovsky, the eminent Russian composer, who has come to this country to direct the production of several of his works at the Music Festival in the city next week, was born in 1840 at Wiatka, in the Ural district of Russia, where his father was engineer to the imperial mines. When the family removed to St. Petersburg ten years later, the lad entered the School of Jurisprudence, and after completing the prescribed course he was appointed to a post in the Department of Justice. This was in 1859, but when three years later Anton Rubinstein founded the Conservatory of Music at St. Petersburg, Tchaikovsky decided to relinquish the law and devote himself to the study of the theory of Music. He made rapid progress, taking his diploma in 1865 and also a prize medal for his Cantata on an ode by Schiller. He was invited by Nicolas Rubinstein[25] to take the post of Professor of Composition in the Conservatory, and discharged its duties until 1877, when a serious nervous affliction caused him to resign the professorship. Teaching was not agreeable to him, and he has since devoted himself entirely to composition, creating for himself a reputation which places him in the front rank of modern composers. In Russia the works of Tchaikovsky are more admired than those of his fellow countryman Rubinstein, and both in England and in USA as well as on the Continent, he is esteemed as a composer of marked originality, whose productions exhibit the striking characteristics of the slavonic temperament. M. Tchaikovsky is a master of the modern orchestra, as is shown in the brilliant effects he produces. He has marked fertility, as well as originality, as a composer, his more important works comprising nine operas and ballets, five symphonies and several symphonic poems, concertos and lesser works for orchestra. Many of these are familiar to N.Y. concert-goers, the Suite No. 3 for orchestra which is to be given during the Festival being one of the most popular. It is a thoroughly characteristic work of the most Russian of Russian composers.

Evening Post, May 2, 1891

"Tchaikovsky," says a writer in the Epoch, "lives very secluded in a small city near Moscow, called Maidanovo. He sees but few persons, and never goes to St. Petersburg or even Moscow unless called there by a rehearsal of his works. He composes while taking long walks always noting down in a little book musical ideas as fast as they come to him, and writing them out when he returns to his house. His principle is to work at any time, believing that inspiration comes with labor. Even though the first inspiration may not be of the highest quality, there is always time enough to reject it upon revision. A great many of the Russian composers, he says, dream and wait for their inspiration, and, as this inspiration does not come as quickly as they desire, they try to aid its coming by drinking, a means that has caused many of them to end tragically. The Russian composer is tall and slender, with a high forehead and long, straight hair, entirely white; his blue large eyes, wellformed nose and mouth, fresh complexion, and moustache, with its upturned points, give to his physiognomy a young look in spite of his white hair . . ."

DIARY   May 2

At 10:15 o'clock I was already at the Music Hall, for the rehearsal. It was held in the big hall amidst noise of workers, beating of hammers, and fuss of managers. The orchestra is seated in the width of the whole vast stage, in consequence of which the sound is bad and unbalanced. These events had a terrible effect on my nerves and several times I felt flashes of rage and a desire to quit everything with a row and run away. With difficulty I played through the suite and the march, but the piano concerto, in consequence of disorder in the music and the fatigue of musicians, was dropped in the middle of the first movement. Came home, terribly tired, took a bath, changed, and went to Mayer's. With him had breakfast again in an Italian restaurant. Slept at home. The pianist Aus der Ohe came at 5 o'clock and played my concerto so unsuccessfully rehearsed this morning. I wrote Napravnik (an answer to his most kind letter).[26] Dined downstairs with aversion. Walked on Broadway. Went to sleep early. Thank God, sleep doesn't abandon me.

PETER TCHAIKOVSKY TO EDUARD NAPRAVNIK

New York, May 2, 1891

My dear, sweet, kind Eduard Francevich,

You can't imagine what a pleasure your letter gave me and how touched I am by your kind attention and remembrance of me. I am terribly, poignantly homesick, and every message from a dear, close man is an invaluable consolation to me.

My trip was quite safe, although for two days an unusually severe hurricane followed us. At some moments it was very frightening. Fortunately I went by one of the most immense steamers of the French steamship line. Due to its colossal dimensions, the tossing was less apparent. Was at sea eight full days.

They greeted me here with unusual cordiality. Nowhere outside of Russia have I seen such a hearty attitude toward foreigners, such a readiness to oblige and serve you in every way. On the day after my arrival there was a rehearsal. The orchestra is very good, especially the woodwinds. It is enlarged—in the first violin section there are eleven stands. The musicians received me with delight. It turns out, I am far better known in America than in Europe, and my compositions are performed much and often. The *Hamlet* Overture which has not yet been played in Moscow, has been played here already many times. Two societies have played the Fifth Symphony two seasons in a row. On the whole I am much more of a big shot here than in Europe. The American lifestyle, habits, and customs are all exceedingly interesting and original. At every step I stumble on phenomena that amaze me by their grandiosity and colossal dimensions as compared to Europe. Life is in full swing here. Although their main interest is profit, the Americans are still very attentive to art. The grand new hall, which was just built and for the opening of which I am invited here, serves as evidence of it. This multimillion-dollar structure is built from music lovers' money. The same rich lovers of music maintain a permanent orchestra. There is nothing of the kind with us! I must confess that the scope and grandiosity of all American undertakings are tremendously appealing to me. I'm also pleased by their constant concern for comfort. My room has, like all rooms in all hotels, electric and gas lighting, a lavatory with a bathtub and basin, a lot of extremely comfortable furniture, an apparatus to speak with the hotel office in case of need, and many other means of comfort which don't exist in Europe. In a word this country is in many respects very ap-

pealing and unusually interesting. I will tell you a great
deal when we meet. I repeat that despite the newness and
intensity of my impressions, the fiercest homesickness
gnaws at me and I yearn for homecoming as for some unattainable good!

The series of concerts will start on the 5th and finish on
the 9th. Then I am off to Niagara; on the 15th and 18th I
have concerts in Philadelphia and Baltimore, and on the
21st I depart. I will write or tell you about the concerts. Colonne's conduct concerning you is inconceivable. He told
me in Paris that he was very interested in making your acquaintance for he has heard much about you. As to the epi-
logue of the tragicomedy with the Music Society, I am not
surprised at all by Anton Grigoryevich's peculiarities and
childish tricks. All that you relate about him is consistent
with his habitual egotism. I regret that the conservatory is
losing the good fortune of having at its head such an intel-
ligent, decent, and talented man as you, but I am very glad
personally for you. No doubt it's easier for you to bear a
burden of theatrical service, to which you are accustomed,
than a conservatory's squabbles. But the threat, that you
will be expelled, is silly. Despite the many troubles that you
have lately suffered in the theater, I know that at the bottom they value you, are afraid of you, and highly esteem
you.

Before my departure to America I wrote to Ivan Alexandrovich that I felt unable to write an opera and ballet for
the next season. I don't regret this at all now, for I see, I'll
not be able to start work before early June. But is it possible to successfully complete such a work by September? It's
evident, that even if I had written something, I would have
done it badly. Tell Olga Eduardovna II (or Varvara Eduardovna) that I feel guilty toward them: I forgot to send a
portrait to the author of the verses. I will bring it from
America. I also feel terribly guilty toward I. A. Melnikov,
but I'll write him personally in a few days!

I kiss Olga Eduardovna's hands, embrace Volodia, Kotia, and you, dear friend.

P. Tchaikovsky

Fondest regards to your young ladies.

DAY EIGHTH

New York Morning Journal, May 3, 1891
Wagner and His Music by P. Tchaikovsky—the noted Russian composer

I am asked to tell the readers of the Morning Journal my opinion of Wagner. I will do so, squarely and frankly. But I must warn them that I recognize two sides to the question: first, Wagner, and the rank he holds among the composers of the Nineteenth Century and secondly, Wagnerism. It will at once be seen that, while I admire the composer I have but little sympathy with what constitutes the cult of Wagnerian theories.

As a composer, Wagner is certainly the most remarkable musical character of the latter part of this century, and his influence upon music is enormous.

He was gifted with great powers of musical invention; he discovered new forms of his art; he led the way into paths until his advent unknown; he was, it may be said, a man of genius, capable of ranking in German music with Mozart, Beethoven, Schubert and Schumann.

But according to my deep and unalterable conviction, he was a genius who followed a wrong path.

Wagner was a great symphonist, but not a composer of opera. Instead of devoting his life to the musical illustration of German mythological characters in the form of opera, had this extraordinary man written symphonies, we should, perhaps, possess masterpieces of that order, worthy rivals to the immortal ones of Beethoven.

All that we admire in Wagner belongs essentially to the symphonic order. That in his music, which leaves a great and profound impression, is now a masterly overture in which he pictures Dr. Faust; or it is the prelude of "Lohengrin," in which the celestial regions for some of the most beautiful pages in modern music; now it is the ride of the Valkyries, the funeral march of "Siegfried," or the blue waves of the Rhine, in the "Rhinegold"—are they not all essentially symphonic? In the "Tetralogy" and "Parsifal" Wagner gives no thought to the singers; in those beautiful and majestic symphonies they are treated as instruments, forming part of the orchestra.

Now, what is Wagnerism? What are the dogmas, which one must profess to be a Wagnerite? One must deny absolutely all that is not of Wagner; it is necessary to ignore Mozart, Schubert, Meyerbeer, Schumann, Chopin; one must be intolerant, exclusive, narrow, extravagant. No! While venerating the sublime genius that created the prelude of "Lohengrin," and the ride of the Valkyries, devoutly kneeling before the prophet—I will not profess the religion he has founded.

PETER TCHAIKOVSKY TO ANATOLY TCHAIKOVSKY

New York, May 3, 1891

Dear Tolia,

Received your two letters. From the second, I found out about the impending change in your place of employment. I am both happy and unhappy about it. If you love Tiflis as much as I do, then I understand how hard it is for you to leave this lovely country, populated by nice people, and move to Jurgenson's homeland. But it's good in that first, this is inevitably leading you to a governorship (in Revel itself) and second, you will be closer to your own people. In summer Revel is charming—all will say so. Am fervently eager to know how your affair will be settled and when you will have to move. Poor Pania! I think it is more painful for her than for you to leave Tiflis.

I will not write a great deal about my stay hereabouts, for I keep a detailed diary of events, which I will bring with me, and after close ones in Petersburg have read it, I will immediately send it to you. They pamper, respect, and indulge me here very much, but I'm terribly bored and homesick. And all of my time, excepting rare hours of solitude, is full of suffering. Fortunately it is not affecting my health. When you read this letter, I will have already left, for the berth on the ship, which departs on May 21st, is already reserved. Oh! I wish this happy moment would come sooner!!! As soon as I set out on my return, the load will be off my mind. Am meeting many people, seeing all the sights, forever astonished by American enterprise and the grandiosity of all their undertakings. When I go to rehearsals, both the orchestra and chorus greet me enthusiastically each time. Now and then I reserve for myself hours of solitude, and, in a word, with difficulty drag out a miserable existence. Such trips are not fitting for my character and age! Letters from Russia are my only consolation. Thank God, Leva, the children, and Nata bear their distress calmly.

And now, I kiss and embrace all of you with all my strength. From this distance my heart burns with deep love for all close ones.

Yours,
P. Tchaikovsky

DIARY   May 3

Dispatch from Jurgenson: "Christ is Risen!" It's raining outside. Letters from Modia and Jurgenson. "No, only he who knew"[27] what it meant to be far from dear ones could know the value of letters. I've never before experienced

anything of the kind. I was visited by Mr. Narrainov and
his wife. He is a tall, bearded, partly greying man, very un-
tidily dressed, who complained of his disease of the spinal
column, speaking Russian not without accent, but well, and
railed against Jews (although he himself smacks of a Jew).
She is a homely English female (sic, not American), who
speaks nothing but English. She brought a stack of newspapers and pointed out her articles in them. Why these people came to me, I don't know. He asked if I'd composed a
fantasy on the "Red Sarafan."[28] At my negative reply he
showed surprise and added: "It's strange! Thalberg composed one but you didn't! As a Russian you must do so. I'll
send you Thalberg's fantasy and please, do it like his!"
I barely got rid of these strange visitors. At 12 o'clock
von Sachs called for me. This elegant little fellow, who
speaks French impeccably, knows music thoroughly, and
treats me so affectionately, is almost the only man in New
York whose company is not burdensome and even pleasant
to me. We walked together through the park. This park,
where the still-not-old Mayer remembers cows once grazed,
is now one of the finest in the world, even though the trees
are comparatively young. At this time of year, when the
trees are covered with fresh green and the lawn is perfectly
groomed, it has a special fascination. At 12:30 we ascended
in an elevator to the fourth floor of a colossal building,
where the apartment of Mr. Schirmer is located. Schirmer
is the local Jurgenson, i.e., owner of the best store and a
first-class publisher. He is 63 years old, but in appearance,
no more than 50. He had been in America since the age of
twelve and, although very much Americanized, still retains
many German habits and is, all in all, a German at heart.
He is very rich and lives not without luxury. With him live
his attractive daughter Mrs. White with her children and
his son with his wife. Schirmer's wife and two younger
daughters have lived two years already in Weimar, where
he had sent the older children to study, for fear that they
might cease to be German. At dinner there were, besides

von Sachs and myself: a local celebrity, the conductor
Seidl[29] (a Wagnerian) and his wife; the pianist Adele Aus
der Ohe (who will play my concerto at the festival) with her
sister; and the Schirmer family. Before dinner we were
treated to some mixture of whiskey, bitters, and lemon—
unusually delicious. The dinner was abundant and very
tasty. On Sunday Schirmer always dines at one o'clock and
likes to toss an extra glass then. The conversation at first
taxed me, but all of Schirmer's family and especially
Mrs. White were so nice, simple, and cordial that by the
end of the dinner things went easier for me. The conductor Seidl told me that next season they're giving my *Maid of
Orleans*.[30] At 4 o'clock I had to be at the rehearsal. They
drove me to the Music Hall in the Schirmer carriage in the
company of von Sachs. Music Hall was illuminated and ti-
died up today for the first time. While the oratorio "Sulamith" by Damrosch the father was going on, I sat in Carnegie's box. Then they sang a boring cantata—"Seven Words"
by Schütz. Then came my turn. My little choruses went off
very well. Quite reluctantly I went again with von Sachs to
Schirmer's, where I'd promised to return. There I found
that a big company had been invited to see me. Schirmer
led us onto the roof of the building in which he lives. The
vast nine-story building has a roof built in such a way that
it provides a fascinating and extensive stroll with views
opening on all four sides. At this time the sun was setting.
It is impossible to describe all the glory of this majestic
spectacle. Having descended, we found only an intimate
circle amidst which I, to my complete surprise, felt quite
content. A. Aus der Ohe played several pieces quite well;
together, she and I played my concerto. At about 9 o'clock
we sat down for supper. At 10:30 we, i.e., von Sachs, Aus
der Ohe, her sister, and I, were supplied with gorgeous
roses, sent down in the elevator, seated in the Schirmer carriage one more time, and conveyed to our homes. To be
fair with respect to Amercian hospitality one must admit:
only in our country can anything like it be found.

DAY NINTH

DIARY   May 4

Received letters from Kolia Conrady, Annette, Sapelnikov, Conius. Drank tea in my room. A visit of Mr. Ro-
meiko, the owner of a newspaper clipping bureau. Very
likely, he is one of our anarchists. Likewise the two mysterious Russians, who yesterday spoke with me at the rehearsal.
Wrote letters and diary. . . .

PETER TCHAIKOVSKY TO NIKOLAY CONRADY[31]

New York, May 4, 1891

My dear Nikolasha,

Just received your letter. No possibility to explain to what
extent letters from near ones, especially informative ones
like yours, please me!!! Thank you!!! I will not write any
particulars to you, for I will bring with me a full diary. I
shall only speak of my feelings. Properly speaking, I have
only one thought and one feeling now: to stay until May 21
when, with all my obligations met, I board the steamer
Fürst Bismarck and set out for Hamburg. All the other
things I try to bear as patiently as possible. The only pleasant hours, rather to say minutes, occur in the evening when
I am alone in my room and have a night and morning
ahead of me that are free from visits. For the remaining
time I feel, in the first place, constantly tired as if I'd gone
on foot about forty miles. They say it's a property of the air
here. Second, more than ever I suffer from the strange
outer world, all the more when I have to speak German
and sometimes even English! But unexpectedly pleasant
hours can also occur. For instance, yesterday I spent the
entire day in the house of the local Jurgenson, that is, the
major music publisher Schirmer. At first I felt the burden
and suffered, but by evening, while amidst unusually dear

and kind people, I suddenly felt at home and content. Truthfully speaking, they are very nice people. And in general I can't sufficiently praise the people and their friendly attitude toward me. Perhaps too nice, for it is too difficult for me to arrange my hours of solitude. I like New York more and more. By the way, there is a magnificent Central Park here. And it's remarkable, that people of my age remember quite well when cows grazed on this place. I have rehearsals almost every day. The new hall where the Festival will be held is splendid and exceeds in dimensions all of ours. On May 10 I go to Niagara, on the 15 conduct in Philadelphia, on the 18th in Baltimore, and on the 21st I leave. The weather is excellent but too hot. All trees have bloomed long ago. How far I am from you! Who knows when you will receive my letter-diary. It is still at sea.

Warmly and fondly, I embrace and kiss you.

Yours—
P. Tchaikovsky

PETER TCHAIKOVSKY TO ANNA MERKLING [32]

New York, May 4, 1891

Golubushka Ania,

I've already received two of your most lovely letters. Letters from dear ones are of such benefit to me now that nothing quite equals them—and always you write so much, so thoroughly, and so interestingly!!!

Since I keep here a detailed diary which I'll bring with me and, naturally, give you to read, I'll not go into any details. But details of my ocean passage you probably knew from Modest, to whom I sent my diary! From that letter you will learn how faithlessly Katu dealt with me and how anxious I was to see her, especially during the first days of the passage. New York, the native inhabitants, the local hospitality and friendliness, the attention and honor accorded to me everywhere—all this pleases me greatly. But all this is so unlike our life and our customs, that I have to write at great length and in great detail in order to give even an approximate notion about America. Therefore I decided to write in diary form the full story of my stay here, which, of course, will be more interesting than fragmentary facts which I would report in separate letters. My frame of mind is, of course, somewhat better than on the first days of my stay in New York. I've already managed to adapt somewhat. But, nevertheless, I can only live by hoping that somehow I'll leave sooner. Unfortunately, it's impossible to go away earlier than May 21. In a week, after finishing off my engagements at the New York Festival, I'll go to Niagara, on the 15th I have a concert in Philadelphia, on the 18th in Baltimore and then—my departure! Oh, blissful minute! No, it's clear that in this life one can only purchase tranquility and happiness—even minutes of happiness—at the price of patience and suffering. Think of yourself! God grant that Peter Ivanovich will find a post so that you will feel relief from present adversities. Ania! I am still looking for some knickknack to buy for you—but not finding it. But I'll think on it until my departure. Tomorrow is the first concert. I am very satisfied with the orchestra and chorus too.

I kiss your hand and Luba's. I embrace Peter Ivanovich and the children.

Yours

DIARY   May 4 (continued)

. . . Having called on Mayer, went to Downtown with him by the elevated. We came for Hyde who led us to breakfast in the Downtown Club. First he took us incredibly high in the elevator and showed us the premises of five lawyers and the law library, that serve his Trust Company. The Downtown Club is nothing other than a superb restaurant, into which they let none but Club members. All of them are commerical people, who are at a distance from their homes, and therefore eat their lunch there. After an excellent breakfast I went on foot along Broadway, alas, with Mayer. This ever-kind German can't understand at all that his sacrifices in the service of me are needless and even a burden for me. What a pleasure it would have been to walk alone! But Mayer is ready to neglect his complicated pursuits if only I wouldn't be alone. So, despite my arguments that he go home and conduct his own business, he dragged along with me for an hour and a half—on foot! From that walk, you can gain a notion of Broadway's length. We walked an hour and a half but barely traversed a third of this street!!! After freshening up in a rest room, we headed for Chickering Hall for the concert of the famous English singer, Santley. The famous singer turned out to be an old man, who, in proper time, very colourlessly sang arias and romances in English, with an English pronunciation and an English erectness and stiffness. I was greeted by various critics including that Fink, who in winter enthusiastically wrote me about *Hamlet*. Before the concert was over I set off home where I had to work at my piano concerto with A. Aus der Ohe. She appeared with her sister and I pointed out to her various nuances, details, and subtleties, which her strong, clear, and brilliant play lacked, judging by the rather coarse performance yesterday. Reno gave me interesting details about Aus der Ohe's American career. She came here four years ago without a penny, but secured an invitation to play Liszt's concerto (whose pupil she is) in the Symphony Society. Her playing was well-liked; invitations poured down from everywhere; everywhere a great success accompanied her; for four years she roamed from city to city, all over America and now she has a capital of half a million marks!!! Such is America! Upon her leaving, hardly had time to change before going to Reno's for dinner. I went on foot and found [Reno's place] without difficulty. For this once we dined in a family circle. Only Damrosch came over after dinner. I played four-hand with likable Alice. The evening passed pleasantly enough. Reno walked me to the tramway. Suddenly began to get very cold.

DAY TENTH

PETER TCHAIKOVSKY TO JULIUS CONIUS[33]

New York, May 5, 1891

My dear friend,

Am writing on business and awfully afraid that my letter will not reach you in Paris. Yesterday, in the company of big local musical bosses, discussed the fact that their major symphony orchestra requires two concertmasters. In hopes of finding them, the conductor Damrosch goes to Europe. It suddenly dawned on me that it would not be bad for you to come here, and I immediately told Damrosch that he would not find anybody better than you. They want concertmaster-soloists. Damrosch became awfully interested in you but he is somewhat embarrassed by your extreme youth. This last circumstance will probably prevent you from becoming the 1st concertmaster but then you can easily be the second. I would strongly suggest that you accept the invitation. You will not believe what an amazing country it is and how easy you, with your talent, can have a tremendous artistic and material success here. The pianist Aus der Ohe, who came here four years ago without a farthing of money, has a fortune of half a million marks now. There are no violinists here to equal you. In ten years you can become a truly rich man. They will definitely offer you quite advantageous terms. Damrosch goes to Berlin in late May (of the new style) and will stay there for three weeks. You can find his address at the American embassy. So, in mid-June be in Berlin, if you please, and seek out Damrosch. I don't know whether the idea of going so far away for several years agrees with you; if it doesn't scare you, go to Berlin and set up your business. Am awfully thankful for your most kind letter. Write me an answer in Russia (city of Klin, Province of Moscow). Embrace you hard.

P. Tchaikovsky

Yesterday I wrote to Sapelnikov in London. I think that you are also in London but have addressed to Paris.

PETER TCHAIKOVSKY TO ALEXEY SOFRONOV

New York, May 5, 1891

Dear friend Alexey Ivanovich,

Forgive me that I am so late in writing you. I have much to do, guests besiege me, and such despair preys upon me that I don't want to undertake anything. And yet, thank God, I am perfectly well. I made my sailing here safely, although for two days there was a terrible storm and my heart was in my mouth from fear. New York is a very big, very interesting city, hardly resembling European cities at all and even less Russian cities. There are quarters where no buildings are fewer than 9 or 10 stories tall. There are buildings with 13 stories!!! The American people are very nice, very hospitable and kind, and I am greatly celebrated here. But it would have been better had they left me more on my own. I count the days and hours until I can return home. The berth on the ship, by which I'll go, is already reserved. I'll leave on May 21—on Nikolin Day itself. By the end of the month I'll be home. Am writing "home" but where is this home—I don't know. I hope that you've thought of writing me and that I'll soon receive news from you. Rehearsals run every day now. Today is the first concert; the last—in five days. Afterwards will go to view the waterfalls of Niagara. Then I'll conduct in Philadelphia and Baltimore, and on the 21st, God willing, I'll leave!!!!

I embrace you, Katia, and bow to Petrovich and Demyanovna.

Yours,
P. Tchaikovsky

You probably know already about Alexandra Ilyinichna's death.

May 5

The servant Max, who brings my morning's tea, spend all his childhood in Nizhnyi-Novgorod and studied in a school there. Since the age of fourteen he has lived in either Germany or New York. Now he is 32 and has forgotten so much Russian that he expresses himself with great difficulty, even though he knows most of the ordinary words. It's pleasant for me to talk a little Russian with him. At 11 o'clock the pianist Rummel appeared (my old Berlin acquaintance) still with the same entreaty that I conduct at his concert on the 17th, for which purpose he'd come once before to me. Then came a reporter—very affable and bland. He asked me whether my wife likes her stay in New York. They have often asked me this question. It turns out, that in some newspapers it was said on the day after my arrival that I came with a young and pretty wife. This happened because two reporters saw me getting into a carriage with Alice Reno, near the steamship dock. Had breakfast downstairs in the hotel. Walked on Broadway. Dropped in at the Viennese cafe recommended to me, but had the misfortune to encounter the conductor Seidl, and was obliged to talk with him. But I had other things on my mind. I was worried about my upcoming first appearance for an evening concert, before an audience of five thousand. Having come home, had the extreme displeasure of receiving Mr. Buso (one of my French fellow travelers) thrown upon me. He stayed endlessly long, affecting a sad appearance as if waiting for me to ask why he was upset. When I at last asked him this question, Buso said that yesterday in Central Park all his money had been lifted and that he came to ask me for 200 francs. And the rich father? And the billions of corks, which are manufactured and sent all over the world? Are all these old wives' tales of his rubbish? I assured him that I have no money now, but probably will give him some at the end of the week. All this is very suspicious and I begin to wonder whether he did not swipe my wallet on the steamer. I will have to deliberate with Reno. At 7:30 Reno's son-in-law dropped by for me.[34] In an overcrowded trolley we approached the Music Hall. Illuminated and filled with an audience, it had unusually impressive and grand appearance. . . .

From the Concert Program:

. . . The engagement of the Russian composer Tchaikovsky adds a very pleasant and original feature to the Festival. He is the greatest representative Russian composer living to-day, sharing with Brahms and Saint-Saens the honors of European fame. He will be heard in several of his own best creations, among them a march, two a capella choruses written in the style of Palestrina and Orlando di Lasso, his Suite No. 3 for orchestra, and his Concerto No. 1 for piano and orchestra. M. Tchaikovsky will also take a prominent part in the Festival, in conducting his own compositions. It will be the first time in America's musical history that a Russian composer will wield the baton. No country in Europe, it may be added, has made such a remarkable advance in music as Russia has during the last three or four decades. The seed-thought of national music sown by Wagner in Germany has apparently taken permanent root in the great empire, and, with the traditional splendor of the music of the Greek church and the folk-songs of the people, has developed wonderful blossoms. . . .

DIARY   May 5 (continued)

. . . I sat in a box with the Reno family. The concert began with Reno's speech (about which the poor fellow was terribly worried before). After him they sang the national hymn. Then a pastor made what was said to be an unusually dull speech in honor of the founders of the edifice, and especially in honor of Carnegie. Next the Leonore Overture was very well performed. Intermission. I came down. Excitement. My turn. Was loudly received. The

March went by very well. Great success. For the rest of the concert I listened from the Hyde's box. "Te Deum" by Berlioz is dullish; only at the end did I taste the intense pleasure of it. The Renos carried me away to their home. An improvised supper. Slept like a dead man.

DAY ELEVENTH

New York Herald, May 6, 1891
Music crowned in its new home
Brilliant inauguration of the Music Hall by the first Festival Concert

Splendid is the new temple of music that was formally inaugurated last night with the first concert of a largely planned festival, and splendid was the audience assembled for an event which marks a new epoch in the musical history, in which one brilliant page now follows the other, of this metropolis. The new Music Hall, for which New York is so largely indebted to the public and artistic spirit of Mr. Andrew Carnegie, is the first thoroughly adequate building to be erected here as the special home of orchestral and choral work.

In the Music Hall, and the Metropolitan Opera House the city now has two temples of music, which in their size and appointments for both performers and public, are not surpassed by those of any city in the world.

The programmes arranged for four evenings and two afternoon performances of the festival enlist the services of a fine array of soloists, of the Symphony Society and the Chorus of the Oratorio Society, both under the direction of Mr. Walter Damrosch, a feature of unusual interest being the first American appearance of the famous Russian composer Peter Tchaikovsky, as the conductor of his own works. . . .

. . . All was bustle outside the big temple of music before

the festival began. The big bright lights outside the entrance to the handsome building threw a strange light in Fifty-seventh street and lit up hundreds of faces. . . . Carriage after carriage rolled up to the broad entrance and deposited its precious freight. . . . At one time there was a line of carriages standing from the entrance to the hall a full quarter of a mile away. . . .

Long before the doors opened the street in front of the hall was crowded with people who wanted to enter. . . . Ladies, whose bonnets must have cost more than the average laborer receives a week for his labor, stood in line waiting for the doors to open. . . . The audience enthusiastically applauded Mr. Andrew Carnegie when he and his party entered their box. Mr. Walter Damrosch also had a warm greeting when he took his place at the conductor's desk. Bishop Potter was introduced in a few suitable words by Mr. Morris Reno, the president of the Music Hall company.

The Bishop spoke at length—at too much length. A hush fell on the audience, broken only by the sound of swinging doors and nervous coughs. . . .

With a sigh of relief, the audience rose and lifted up its thousand voices to the tune of "America." The trained choir on the platform led the anthem. . . .

After that "we had some music." The audience sat down and Mr. Damrosch got up, and the next moment our expectant ears were ravished by the sublime strain of the Leonore overture.

The acoustics. That was our first thought. Our minds were soon relieved on that score. The building had been admirably planned. So far at all events, as we could judge from the orchestra, the acoustics were perfect: there was no echo, no undue reverberation. Each note was heard. The orchestral combinations were not blurred or exaggerated. The overture seemed more than usually grand. It was played with admirable feeling, and spirit. Mr. Damrosch proved an excellent conductor. And so after the last notes of the wondrous composition died away there were two rounds of applause and then a third, as the composer, Tchaikovsky, was seen emerging from the back of the stage to direct the execution of his march. . . .

Tchaikovsky is a tall, gray, well built, interesting man, well on the sixty. He seems a trifle embarrassed, and responds to the applause by a succession of brusque and jerky bows. But as soon as he grasps the baton his self-confidence returns. There is no sign of nervousness about him as he taps for silence. He conducts with the authoritative strength of a master and the band obeys his lead as one man.

His "Marche Solennelle" is simple, strong and sober, but not surprisingly original. The leading theme recalls that "Hallelujah" chorus, and the treatment of the first part is Handelian. The strings for some time have things to themselves. Then the orchestration grows more rich and varied, as the cymbals, the brass and the woodwinds join in. And at last we return to the original theme, working gradually up to a grand climax in which all the instruments take part. Of the deep passion, the complexity and poetry which mark some other works of the composer's—his "Romeo" overture for instance—there is no sign in this march. It is a broad, scholarly and worthy effort. But a dozen other men might have produced it.

The Berlioz "Te Deum" closed the programme. . . .

Morning Journal, May 6, 1891
Music's new home

The formal opening of the new Music Hall, at Seventh avenue and Fifty-seventh street, last night was an event long to be remembered.

The Hall was filled to overflowing with a brilliant and appreciative audience. All of the sixty-two boxes were filled with lovely women in beautiful gowns glistening with jewels that vied with the thousands of electric lights. The parquet also presented a similar scene, of rare beauty and brilliancy, and all seemed to be imbued with the spirit of the place.

The walls of the new building almost shook when that grand old chorale, "Old Hundredth" was sung by the Oratorio Chorus, as one mighty voice of praise and thanksgiving for the beautiful and permanent home music will henceforth have in this city. . . .

The dedication services conducted by the Rt. Rev. Henry C. Potter, D.D., consisted of an address depicting the struggle of music in this city from the time of the foundation of the Philharmonic Society some fifty years ago until to-night when its efforts were crowned by success.

Nothing that Bishop Potter said in the praise of the building was too much. It certainly is one of the handsomest in this city. The entrance to it is guarded by tall, gray corinthian pillars, and the vestibule, with beautiful mosaic dado, reflecting numerous electric lights is beautiful.

Entering the music hall proper, its size and architectural purity fill one with a felling somewhat akin to awe. Its proportions are perfect and the coloring chaste, the treatment of the decorations being much like that of the Metropolitan Opera House. . . .

The Marche Solennelle, by Tchaikovsky, was conducted by the eminent composer himself. Mr. Tchaikovsky has a wonderful personality and seems to have thoroughly suffused the orchestra with his slavonic enthusiasm, for it rendered the Marche Solennelle admirably. If at times Tchaikovsky sacrifices the ideal for the wild and fantastic, he does so with a power that at once enchains us and charms us by the splendor of his oriental coloring, his subtleness and his wonderful imagery. . . .

New York Tribune, May 6, 1891
The Music Hall opened

Tchaikovsky received a royal welcome when he stepped forward to lead the orchestra after the intermission. The piece was the "March Solennelle," and he was compelled to respond with an encore. . . .

Mr. Tchaikovsky long ago conquered recognition for his genius in New York. We have spoken of his representative character, and he is indeed in a particular sense an exemplar of Russian art. Three years ago, he visited the chief cities of Western Europe, at the direct insistence, or at least through the direct mediation of the Russian Government. A travelling stipend was given to him that he might exhibit the traits of the wonderful progress which Russia has made in music within scarcely more than a generation. Wherever he went he was the hero of the hour and through his agency, the people of Paris, London and other European capitals, came to realize the force of Von Bulow's remark many years ago, that the best German music was now being written in Paris and St. Petersburg. It is not necessary to accept this dictum as literally true to see its forcefulness. There are still composers in Germany whose works suffer nothing when compared with the best products of the Russian school, but the aggressiveness of Mr. Tchaikovsky and his colleagues, their marvellous daring and mastery of those elements of composition, which proclaim creative vigor, the newness, strangeness and dramatic potency of the folk music whose spirit they infuse into their compositions even when they make no use of their popular melodies all combine to justify the belief that the dominant school of the last 100 years has a dangerous rival in these Slavonic composers. . . .

In Russia the great heart of the people rests in the music even of such cultured and finished composers as Mr. Tchaikovsky and it therefore has an elemental power. There is a trace of barbarism in it with its directness, truthfulness and forcefulness. Mr. Tchaikovsky is an interesting phenomenon in our present activities because in him we are constrained to see the wise mediator between the staid German school and the reckless, untamed zeal of the younger men among his colleagues, like Rimsky-Korsakov, who would sacrifice the essence of art for the sake of national feeling. He is also interesting because of all the Russian musicians except Rubinstein, we know his music best. The evening was full of delights, to which the festive feeling inspired by the chaste lines and colors of the hall and the lovely picture presented by the chorus lent a very considerable help. Not the least remarkable feature was the smoothness with which the prearranged order of exercises was carried out. There was no interruption, and applause was distributed with great impartiality whenever a reference was made by the orator of the evening to the man and institutions which have been notable in the musical activities of the past. The heartiest burst of applause, however, was that which greeted Mr. Tchaikovsky when he came upon the stage to conduct his March Solonnelle. His bearing was modest but unconstrained, his beat firm but undemonstrative. The orchestra started the glad acclaim with fanfare, and after he laid down the baton he was recalled again and again to bow his acknowledgements. His March proved to be a sonorous composition, of strong and simple outlines, scored with the consummate mastery noticeable in all of his compositions for orchestra. In the Coda a splendid climax is worked up by the introduction of a phrase from the Russian National Hymn, an element which is almost inevitable in the marches and festival overtures of the men of Tchaikovsky's school.

Evening Post, May 6, 1891
The new Music Hall

May 5 will always be a memorable day in the annals of music in America as being the date on which a new Music Hall was dedicated which will doubtless be the centre of our musical life for a century to come, and on which, moreover, one of the greatest composers of the nineteenth century made his first appearance before an American audience—a composer whose name will be more and more conspicuous on our concert programmes as years go on. . . . The climax of the last evening's performance was of course the appearance of M. Tchaikovsky to conduct his festival march. All the applause previously bestowed, warm as it was, seemed pianissimo, compared with the demonstration of welcome accorded to the eminent Russian Composer. Again and again he had to bow his acknowledgements, and at the end he was recalled repeatedly and unanimously. He looks somewhat older than he is, owing to his white hair, but the fire in his eyes, his energetic actions, and still more the creative spontaneity of his latest works prove that he has only half a century behind him. He conducted his piece without many gestures, but there is a vigorous decisiveness about his beat which compels the band to follow his intentions, and when it is reinforced by the left hand it becomes imperious and irresistible. M. Tchaikovsky is one of the few firstclass composers who have also been great conductors. His march is an imposing composition, in the style of Wagner's Huldingungs and Kaiser March, original in thematic material, rich in orchestration, and majestic in effort, with a touch of national color. His mode of conducting this piece roused great expectations as to his next appearances, on Thursday afternoon, Friday evening, and Saturday afternoon.

The Sun, May 6, 1891
The first night of the music festival

. . . After the intermission Herr Tchaikovsky, the Russian composer, who is the lion and hero of the festival, was introduced to the public, which gave him the most cordial possible greeting and listened to his Marche Solennelle with evidence of special interest. Tchaikovsky is a genial looking and gentlemanly appearing man with a bright complexion, gray hair and beard, and a quick, decided manner, which is emphasized and accentuated while he is conducting. It is good to watch his earnest, energetic movements, each one of which is full of decision and meaning, utterly free from consciousness or affectation. . . .

New York Times, May 6, 1891
The first concert in the new Music Hall

. . . After an intermission of seven or eight minutes, Peter Ilyich Tchaikovsky, the famous Russian composer, one of the high figures of the music of to-day, made his appearance on the stage. He was greeted as he deserved to be and conducted his spirited, militant March Solonnelle, in which the theme of the Russian national hymn is admirably employed.

The Press, May 6, 1891
Carnegie Music Hall opened

. . . Tchaikovsky, the famous Russian composer who ranks fairly with Rubinstein, Dvorak, Brahms and Saint-Saens as one of the half dozen greatest living musicians, was royally received when he took his position to conduct his Solemn March.

He is a fine looking man of 55 or thereabouts, erect in carriage, and with nearly white hair and beard, who exercised excellent control over the band and gave a clear, firmly marked reading to his strongly written march. He was recalled again and again by the enthusiastic applause of the audience, which thus paid a just tribute to one of the first of musicians, a leader of the modern Russian school of music and a man of a great and unquestioned genius. . . .

DIARY   May 6

"Tchaikovsky is a tall, gray, well built, interesting man, well on the sixty (?!!). He seems a trifle embarrassed and responds to the applause by a succession of brusque and jerky bows. But as soon as he grasps the baton his self-confidence returns." That is what I read today in the *Herald*. It angers me that they write not only about the music but about my person, too. I cannot abide when others notice my embarrassment and are surprised at my "brusque and jerky bows."

Started for the rehearsal at 10:30 on foot. With difficulty found the entrance to the hall, through the aid of a workman. The rehearsal went off very well. At the end of the suite the musicians shouted a sort of "hoch." Wholly steeped in perspiration, I had to talk with Mrs. Reno, her oldest daughter, and two other ladies. In Reno's office. A ship's ticket and instructions, concerning my trip to Philadelphia and Baltimore. After changing, hurried to Mayer, where Rummel had waited for me a whole hour and half to play through my Second Concerto. And still we didn't play it, but instead I exercised my eloquence, i.e., proved that I have no cause to accept his proposal to conduct gratis some concert on the 17th. Had breakfast with Mayer in an Italian restaurant. Slept at home. At about 7 o'clock P. S. Botkin appeared unexpectedly from Washington. He came purposely for the concert. At 7:30 Hyde and his wife drove to get me. Second concert. The oratorio "Elijah" by Mendelssohn was performed. Beautiful but somehow long-winded thing. During intermission was dragged to boxes of the various big shots of this place. Carnegie (likable millionaire, founder of the Music Hall) invited me to dine at his home Sunday, but I couldn't accept for I have to go to Mr. Smolls's out in a suburb for the entire day. Having disposed of everyone, I went home on foot. Had supper in the restaurant downstairs. Letters from Modia and brother Kolia. A big fire somewhere.

DAY TWELFTH

DIARY   May 7

My 51st year. Awfully excited this morning. The concert with the suite lies before me at 2 o'clock. A surprising thing is this peculiar fright. How many times have I conducted this very suite! It goes beautifully. What's to be afraid of? And yet I am suffering unbearably!

My sufferings proceeded in crescendo. It seems I have never been so afraid. Is it because they will heed my appearance here and at that point my shyness will show itself? For good or ill after enduring a few difficult hours (partic-

ularly the last, when I was forced to hold conversation with
Mrs. Mielke,[35] etc., while waiting to come out), I came out,
was again splendidly received, and, as it's said in today's
newspapers, made a sensation. After the suite I sat in Reno's office and gave audiences to reporters (ah, these reporters!) including, by the way, the very famous Jackson.
Went up to the box of Mrs. Reno, who sent me a mass of
flowers this morning as if in foreknowledge that today is
my birthday. Feeling the necessity for being alone, I
squeezed my way through the crowd of ladies who surrounded me in the corridor and goggled at me with eyes in
which, unwittingly but with pleasure, I read rapt sympathy,
then passed up invitations from the Reno family, and ran
home. Here, I wrote a message to Botkin that I can't dine
with him as I'd promised; then, relieved and happy as
much as could be, headed off to roam, dine, drop into
cafes,—in short, devoted myself to the enjoyment of silence
and solitude. Retired very early.

DAY THIRTEENTH

New York World, May 8, 1891
Tchaikovsky's ovation at the Music Festival

The third concert of the Festival yesterday afternoon at the
Carnegie Music Hall was in many respects the most interesting yet given. It was made especially so by the production of
Suite No. 3, by Tchaikovsky, led by the Russian Composer
himself, who received an ovation such as has been rarely given
to a great musician in this country. Tchaikovsky's Suite No.
3 has the magnitude of a Symphony. It is made up of a series of four numbers and lasts altogether nearly an hour.
Each number is of rare interest and strange musical beauty.

The Suite begins with a quaint and melodious motive, the
memory, perhaps, of a Russian folktune, and this is brought
back again and again in a hundred different colors and forms.

Such a work needs to be heard several times before it can possibly come to full and clear appreciation; but heard yesterday as it was interpreted under the magnetic and magnificient conducting of the composer, it produced an overwhelmingly great effect.

In a chat with the Russian composer after the concert it was learned with surprise, that he is only to remain in this country two weeks longer and not a full year, as was originally announced. He expressed himself as much delighted with his reception in New York. "Americans," he said, "remind me much in their genial wide-heartedness and splendid hospitality of Russians, and I am glad to be here just now in a sort of semi-representative character and to find that I am the recipient of a welcome that can only come from oldtime friendly diplomatic relations between the Empire and the great Republic. I am sorry that Russia's intellectual life and progress are not better known here than they are, but I myself am so charmed with America and Americans that I am sure I shall wish to do my duty in making America acquainted with Russian musical progress in the future. I trust that this may not be my last visit to America. No. I am not old. I celebrate my fifty-first birthday today. My hair is gray, and the work of conducting makes great calls upon my vitality, but I hope I may often be permitted to enjoy the honors that American audiences are so willing to give me."

The rest of the programme was conducted by Walter Damrosch, to whom it should not be forgotten that the presence of Russia's representative composer is due. It is a difficult task for any other conductor to shine where such a man as Tchaikovsky has a place in the programme.

Evening Post, May 8, 1891
The Music Festival

Large audiences continue to be attracted to the New Music Hall partly by the programmes, and perhaps still more by a desire to enjoy a performance of a Tchaikovsky composition under the composer's direction.

. . . The sensation of the afternoon was M. Tchaikovsky's third suite. It may be stated that the pieces by this composer given at the festival are of his own selection, nor could a better choice than this suite have been made, for it is one of his most inspired and characteristic works.

When the Festival scheme was first made public regrets were expressed that M. Tchaikovsky should not have chosen one of his five symphonies for the occasion. But this suite is almost as elaborate a work as a symphony, and is a very different thing from the sequence of four or more simple dance pieces in the same key, which was called a suite in the seventeenth and eighteenth centuries. Indeed, it approximates the symphony in character, the first and second number representing the opening fast and slower movements, while the third, with its quaint and delightful wood-wind scoring, has decidedly the character of a scherzo. The remainder of the suite shows why the composer preferred to make this a suite rather than a symphony. He obviously did not wish to be hampered by formal fetters which would have hindered him from giving this part a rhapsodic character which, not only in the violin cadenza and solo which Mr. Dannreuther played so well, but in other respects, suggests Liszt.

There is also in the movement a passage which in its dynamic treatment suggests "Tristan." But these are the only things in which M. Tchaikovsky's composition recalls any other master, apart from a general resemblance to his former teacher, Rubinstein, in the broad cantabile and certain oriental intervals which are peculiar to the Russian school. Tchaikovsky's music in a word, is original, unique, and full of local color, the counterpart of the fresh literary spirit which pervades the works of Turgeneff and Tolstoi. As Chopin turned the Polish streams of melody into the main current of European music, and Liszt the Hungarian, so Tchaikovsky and Rubinstein have enriched it with the Russian tributaries. The importance of this work will be more and more appreciated as time goes on, and would be even if these two Russians were not the creative geniuses they are. Both of them were nourished by the great native melodies of their country quite as much as by the pabulum afforded by the great German composers; and how much rich food there is in the popular melodies of Russia may be inferred from the admission of a German writer, A. Melts, that the Russians have a larger number of beautiful folk songs than even the Germans; and the best of them are in the minor mode which makes them particularly palatable to us who have been brought up by Wagner and Chopin to prefer our music in minor keys, which allow greater freedom of modulation, than in major.

That M. Tchaikovsky and his magnificent suite were most enthusiastically applauded need not be said. It would be a great treat if he could be induced to give a concert of his own compositions after the festival, or, rather, after his return from the Baltimore and Washington festivals, in which he participates. In the meantime we look forward with great pleasure to the singing of his two unaccompanied choruses this evening, and his pianoforte concerto in b-flat minor tomorrow afternoon.

Morning Journal, May 8, 1891
Music warm and strong

Although not the first number on the programme of yesterday's Music Festival, the place of honor must be accorded to Tchaikovsky's Third orchestral suite—a marvelous production. Unlike some of the younger members of the Russian school while his music is thoroughly characteristic of his race, Tchaikovsky does not serve up the slavonic folk song in its crude, barbaric state.

Instead he gives us a train of beautiful thoughts, like a gorgeous pageant, at times startling in its effects. Sometimes full of the warm sensuousness of the East, glowing with rich Oriental coloring, and anon assuming the wild fantastic outlines of the North.

Bold, to the extent of daring, it is full of surprises, notably in the last movement. Russian music certainly threatens that of Germany. Yesterday's programme was decidedly peculiar, and except for the selections from Mozart, represented only the extremely modern schools, the German, the Russian and the French. . . .

Brooklyn Daily Eagle, May 8, 1891
The Music Festival

The afternoon concert at the New York music festival yesterday drew a large and enthusiastic audience, notwithstanding that the chorus was not employed; but the soloists were of the best, and the orchestra under Tchaikovsky did some brilliant work. Indeed, Tchaikovsky's orchestral Suite No. 3 was the feature of the concert, a fresh, fascinating work, filled with the modern spirit yet rich in melody, and played with a fire which Mr. Damrosch was not able to evoke from his orchestra. . . .

Evening Telegram, May 8, 1891
Tchaikovsky conducted

. . . The next number was Suite No. 3, for orchestra, by Tchaikovsky, conducted by the composer. It is a splendid work deliciously melodic in parts, with marvellous variations, and ending with a magnificent and inspiring Polonaise. The orchestra did a splendid work, which must have been a surprise to the members themselves. It would be impossible to play badly under such a conductor. Tchaikovsky's leading was a perfect revelation. He inspires his orchestra with his nervous force, and seems to hold every musician at the end of his baton. He roused the audience to a pitch of enthusiasm seldom witnessed. . . .

The Press, May 8, 1981
Mr. Damrosch's third concert

. . . Mr. Tchaikovsky must think that the Americans are a very impressionable people. He has been most cordially received, and yesterday's demonstration was if anything, more heartily and honestly spontaneous than that of the opening night. He conducted his beautiful Suite with the authority and precision of a thorough musician, and was cheered to the echo at its close, the tribute being as much to the composer as to the conductor.

DIARY   May 8

Am beginning to have difficulty finding time for writing letters and this diary. Visitors besiege me: reporters, composers, librettists, one of whom, a little old man,—brought me an opera, *Wlast,* and moved me very much with the story of the death of his only son; but chiefly—whole piles of letters from every corner of America with requests for autographs, to which I very conscientiously respond. Was at the rehearsal of the piano concerto. Was angry at Damrosch, who, taking all the best time, gives me the leftover part of the rehearsal. And yet the rehearsal went off all right. Having changed at home, breakfasted alone at about 3 o'clock. Visited Knabe. He and Mayer were at Martelli's (where I found them in a company drinking champagne); thanked both of them for the splendid present, given to me yesterday (a Statue of Liberty). But how can this thing be allowed into Russia? Hurried home. Visitors are endless, including two Russian ladies. The first of them: Mrs. Mac-Gahan, the widow of the famous correspondent at the time of the war of 1877, and herself the correspondent of the *Russkie Vedomosti* and *Severny Vestnik.* Just when I had my first occasion to have a heart-to-heart talk with a Russian woman,—a painful thing happened. Suddenly tears came, my voice began to tremble, and I couldn't restrain my sobs. I ran out into the other room and for a long time didn't come out. Am burning with shame remembering this unexpected thing. The other lady was Mrs. Neftel, speaking about her husband, Dr. Neftel, as if everyone should know who he is. But I don't know. There was also Mr. Weiner, the president of a chamber music society (with flute), with whom I'd corresponded from Tiflis. Slept a little before the concert. My little choruses went well, but were I less embarrassed and worried, they would have gone better. Sat in the boxes of Reno and Hyde during the performance of the beautiful oratorio "Sulamith" by Damrosch, the father. On the way to supper at Damrosch's, I walked with Reno and Carnegie. This little arch-millionaire is awfully kind to me and was all the time talking about an invitation for the next year. There was a very original supper at Damrosch's. The men went to the table alone and the poor ladies stayed at a distance. The supper was copious, but the cuisine was American, i.e., unusually distasteful. We drank a lot of champagne. I sat in between the host and the concertmaster, Dannreuther. Speaking with him about his brother, I must have seemed either crazy or a desperate liar during the whole two hours. He sat with mouth open in surprise and was perplexed. It turned out that I'd confused in my memory Dannreuther, the pianist, with Hartvigson, the pianist. My absent-mindedness becomes unbearable and, it seems, attests to my old age. By the way, all the gathering was surprised when I said that yesterday I'd reached 51. Carnegie was especially surprised; they all thought (except those who knew my biography) that I was much older. Have I grown old lately? Quite possibly. I feel something in me has gone to pieces. I was driven in the Carnegie carriage. Influenced by talk of my aged appearance, I saw dreadful dreams the whole night long. [In the original ten lines are crossed out.] On a gigantic rocky slope I rolled unceasingly down to the sea clutching at a small jut of some cliff. I believe all this mirrors yesterday's talk of my old age.

Mr. Romaiko sends me every day heaps of newspaper clippings about myself. Without exception they are all laudatory in the highest degree. They exalt to the skies my Third Suite, and my conducting perhaps even more. Do I really conduct so well? Or do the Americans overdo it too much?!!!

DAY FOURTEENTH

Evening Post, May 9, 1891

The Music Festival

The first number on yesterday's programme at the Music Hall appealed to specialists rather than to the general public. It was a performance—the first time in America—of the "Seven Words" by Heinrich Schutz, a famous composer of the seventeenth century. . . .

Apart from such historic points of view, there is little of interest in Schutz's work, except in the unaccompanied choruses. . . . Choral writing was the strong point of the composers preceding Schutz, and little advance has been made in that line within the last two centuries. This was illustrated by the singing of two short unaccompanied choruses by M. Tchaikovsky, immediately after the "Seven Words." Like everything the eminent Russian has written, these choruses are interesting and they were warmly applauded. Yet they might have been almost written by Schutz, whereas between the "Symphonies" or instrumental interludes in the "Seven Words," and Tchaikovsky's suite that was played on Thursday, even an unmusical person, could realise in a minute that there is a world of difference—more than two centuries of evolution. The comparison is suggestive, and helps to explain why the orchestra plays such a prominent role in our musical life at present. . . .

Morning Journal, May 9, 1891

Chorus singing without orchestra at the Festival

Last night was essentially the religious night of the Musical Festival, the programme consisting of "The Seven Words of Our Savior" by Henry Schutz; two a capella choruses of Tchaikovsky, and a sacred cantata entitled "Sulamith" by the late Dr. Leopold Damrosch. . . . Since Wagner is dead there is no question that Tchaikovsky ranks foremost among living composers. That was proven on Thursday when he conducted his Third Suite for Orchestra, a wonderful work. His two a capella choruses, heard for the first time in America, are wonderfully fine compositions, full of deep religious feeling, at times assuming the gorgeous pomp of the Greek ritual, again the mysticism which shrouds the Eastern church and anon the simplicity of the Russian peasant's childlike faith.

Both choruses, the "Pater Noster" and the "Legend," were magnificently sung.

New York Times, May 9, 1891
The Music Hall concerts

. . . The two a capella choruses of Tchaikovsky, a "Pater Noster" and a "Legend," produced under the direction of the composer last night, are new and have not been before heard here. Both exhibit the strong musical feeling and skill of the composer. . . . The two a capella choruses of Tchaikovsky were sung excellently. The first lost much of its effect from the similarity of its color to that of Schutz's music. The "Legend," however, made a great hit. It is characteristic Russian music and the color is delightful. Tchaikovsky was called out twice after it with great enthusiasm. . . .

DIARY   May 9

The weather has become tropical. Max, that most lovely German from Nizhnyi-Novgorod, arranged my apartment so that it appears ideally comfortable. No doubt it's impossible anywhere in Europe to have such indescribable comfort and peace in a hotel. He has added two tables and vases for the masses of flowers sent to me, and also rearranged the furniture. To my dismay, it comes just before the beginning of my wanderings. In general I detect a curious difference between the attitude of all the hotel employees at the beginning of my stay and now. At first they treated me with that coldness and slightly insulting indifference that

verge on hostility. Now everyone smiles, all are ready to
run to the end of the earth at my first word, and even
young men, attached to the elevator, speak to me about the
weather on each of my journeys up or down. But I am far
from convinced that all this is the result of tips, which I
hand out quite generously. No, even without that, all servants are very grateful when they receive friendly treatment. I was visited by Messrs. Mowson and Smith, repre-
sentatives of the Composer's Club, who are about to give a
musical evening, dedicated to my works. Dear Mrs. White
sent me such an abundance of marvelous flowers that after
filling up vases and room I had to present them to Max,
who became ecstatic, for his wife adores them. I was also
visited by the violinist Rietzel, who came for my portrait
and related how the orchestra musicians had grown fond of
me. That moved me very much. After changing I went to
Mayer with that other big portrait. From there to Schirmer,
and then—impetuously to the Music Hall, where my last
appearance before an audience was due. These visits before
the concert show how little I was worried this time. Why? I
have no idea. In the Artist's Chamber I made the acquaintance of the singer who sang yesterday my romance, "Both
Painful and Sweet." A wonderful singer and a lovely
woman. My concerto, perfectly performed by Adele Aus der
Ohe, went off splendidly. There was enthusiasm of a kind
that never arises even in Russia. They called for me again
and again, shouted "upwards," waved their handkerchiefs—
in a word it was evident that I am greatly loved by the
Americans. But especially previous to me was the delight of
the orchestra. In consequence of the heat, the copious
sweat caused by it, and my waving of the baton, I was unable to stay at the concert, and, to my regret, didn't hear
the scene from *Parsifal.* At home took a bath and changed.
Breakfasted (or dined) at five o'clock at my place downstairs. At the final evening concert of the festival I sat in
turn in the boxes of Carnegie, Hyde, Smolls, and Reno.
The oratorio "Israel in Egypt" by Handel was performed

completely, and the performance was excellent. In the middle of the concert an ovation for the architect of the building. After the concert went with Damrosch to von Sachs's for supper. This luxurious supper was given at the Manhattan Club. The building is grand and luxurious. We sat in a separate hall. Although the cuisine of this club is famous, I found it distasteful. On a delicate vignette-menu a little piece of some composition of mine was written for all those invited. Besides myself and Damrosch, guests included the pianist von Suten, the Hungarian Korbay, Rudolph Schirmer, von Sachs's brother, and, finally, the quite famous, quite respected, and loved Schurtz. Schurtz, the friend of Kossuth, Hertzen, and Mazzini, fled Germany in '48. Bit by bit he acquired an important name and achieved a senatorship. The man is indeed very clever, educated and interesting. He sat next to me and spoke a good deal about Tolstoy, Turgenev, Dostoyevsky. On the whole the supper passed very gaily and that was no lack of consideration for me. We broke up at 2 o'clock. The Hungarian Korbay walked me to the hotel.

PETER TCHAIKOVSKY TO MODEST TCHAIKOVSKY

New York, May 9, 1891

Modia,

I begin to have difficulty in finding time for writing letters. Mornings, during free minutes I write in my diary. Today my New York affair is coming to an end. So far I have had tremendous success; the Suite was especially well liked. The press sings hallelujahs to me that I could never dream to hear in Russia. During intermissions and after concerts, ladies gather in crowds to gape at me; others come up and express their delight. Everyone is awfully kind to me. The time is beginning to pass quickly, and already in a week and a half I hope to leave. Today and tomorrow I am faced with difficult days, that is, no single minute of freedom; but then on Monday I go alone to Ni-agara. Afterwards I'll be traveling so much from city to city that I hope my day of departure will arrive unnoticed. My birthday I spent well—at least, the second part of the day. Through the first part I suffered from excitement and fear over my conducting the Suite at a matinee, but after the tremendous success of it I got rid of all invitations and spent the remaining day alone.

Yesterday I was visited by two Russian ladies, who live here. One of them, the first, so touched me by her Russian face and Russian talk, that I burst into tears quite unex-pectedly and now am ashamed and tormented over this reminiscence. It shows you how precious the company of K. I. Laroche, whose most kind letter I received yesterday, would have been for me. In general, I can't complain for lack of letters. Thank you all. Brother Kolia wrote me a charmingly sweet letter. A serious conversation is in pro-gress concerning my engagement for the next season. Ob-viously, the terms will be very advantageous. Shall I get it? If so, I will bring Ziloty and Sapelnikov with me.

Please, give the second letter to brother Kolia. I hope that you will wait for me in Peter[sburg]. Try to persuade Kolia not to leave till my arrival.

Good-bye! I embrace you all hard. Tell Bob that his lovely letter has reached me.

Yours—
P. Tchaikovsky

PETER TCHAIKOVSKY TO NIKOLAI TCHAIKOVSKY

New York, May 9, 1891

Dear friend Nikolasha,

Received your nice and dear letter three days ago and since then couldn't find the time to answer yet. The longer the time is, the more it is absorbed by rehearsals, concerts, receptions, and visits by and to hospitable Americans. Modest probably related to you brief news about me. I am now keeping a detailed diary which upon my arrival will give you to read. In a brief letter one can't say everything. In general I am very pleased with my American welcome; I am respected very much and pampered here. But nevertheless I regret that I came here. I think this voyage will age me very much. I am quite healthy in body, but in spirit—not at all. It's very difficult for me to sojourn amidst a strange people, who speak to me in a strange language. I long for Russia and close ones so much, and nothing rejoices me. I am satisfied only when I manage staying in solitude, but with every day it becomes more difficult. And yet, upon finishing all my engagements in New York I intend to take a two-day tour to Niagara. Then concerts in Philadelphia and Baltimore will come, and on the 21st I will leave. When you receive this letter, I will be at sea already—Lord willing.

I have had great success here. Everyone exalts me, and the press extols in unison most enthusiastically. There is discussion of my being invited for the next year. If terms are very advantageous, I'll probably accept it. But in that case I'll on no account go alone: I must take someone with me. Concerning New York and America in general I will not greatly elaborate, for this subject is so broad that it is impossible to tell all in a brief letter. All that I see here astounds me by its grandiosity of dimensions, scope, and boldness of undertaking. New buildings for instance are built no less than 13 stories high. One new hotel has 17. In Chicago they went even further: they built a building with 21 stories!!!! And everything is done on the same scale. American comfort delights me too. But you will learn everything from my diary. I will come to you in Ukolovo without fail. In Peter[sburg] I'll unfortunately no longer be able to find you.

I embrace you and Olia warmly. Also I fondly kiss my

golubchik George and thank him for his little letter. My God, how I'll be glad to see all of you!

Yours—
P. Tchaikovsky

In your letter you didn't give the number of your house, and I was forced to address this to Modest.

DAY FIFTEENTH

New York World, May 10, 1891
The end of the Festival—M. Tchaikovsky has another ovation at the Music Hall

The Music Festival at the Carnegie Hall came to its conclusion last night with a performance of Handel's oratorio "Israel in Egypt," which had been preceded by a matinee concert of more varied character. During the entire cycle the attendance has been uninterruptedly large, but yesterday afternoon saw one of the most crowded audiences of the week. The special matinee attractions were M. Tchaikovsky as conductor of his First Concerto, played by Miss Adele Aus der Ohe; Beethoven's Fifth Symphony, two songs, and the Prelude and a scene from Wagner's "Parsifal."

The enthusiasm of the afternoon went, of course, to the Russian guest, who, with Miss Aus der Ohe, was called out seven or eight times.

It is the first time in New York musical history that a European composer of the very highest rank has been specially invited to a musical festival here to produce some of his own works, and Mr. Walter Damrosch deserves the sincerest thanks of the New York audiences for enabling them to hear Mr. Tchaikovsky, a composer whom he ranks with Brahms and Saint-Saens but whom we should be inclined to place higher. Some people have even styled the week's cycles a Tchaikovsky Festival.

The festival has in truth been made memorable by Mr. Tchaikovsky's appearance at four concerts out of the six, and it is quite certain that if another series of concerts were arranged for the production especially of the works of the Russian guest that festival would be a great success. But in all this it must be remembered that Mr. Damrosch, with praiseworthy modesty, was the one to invite Mr. Tchaikovsky to grace the festival and to share the honors of a festal occasion, which rightly belonged to him. Mr. Damrosch has shown the true art-spirit in doing this thing and he will properly value the great mission to which he has been called by fortune in New York, if he continues in the way he has so auspiciously begun. . . .

The appearance upon the stage of Mr. Tchaikovsky, when he came forward with Fraulein Adele Aus der Ohe, to conduct his Concerto in b-flat minor, was the signal as here before for prolonged applause. The first few bars of the opening "Andante" proclaimed conductor and pianist in rapport. Miss Aus der Ohe possesses in a marked degree the splendid vitality and verve which are such eminent and enjoyable characteristics in the conducting of Tchaikovsky, a better interpreter could hardly have been chosen, and Miss Aus der Ohe gave proof that she played the work Con Amore. Mr. Tchaikovsky is possessed of rare magnetism, and it is not surprising that the pianist should have felt this, as she came under the influence and direction of his conducting. He carried her along as he carries the orchestra and as he carries and sways his audiences with his orchestral music. . . .

New York Daily Tribune, May 10, 1891
Last of Festival concerts

Mr. Tchaikovsky, who has monopolized individual interest in the festival, conducted the accompaniment to a performance of his B-flat minor Pianoforte Concerto, played by Miss Aus der Ohe, in the afternoon and made it the most brilliant feature of the scheme. It has been heard several times in our concertrooms and each time with more ruggedness and eloquence than the fair player displayed yesterday, though perhaps never with more elegance and devotion. Naturally it evoked a tempest of enthusiasm, which Miss Aus der Ohe, though constrained by Mr. Tchaikovsky to appear each of the several times to acknowledge the gladsome tributes, with graceful modesty insisted was the guerdon of the composer. The other numbers of the programme were Beethoven's Fifth Symphony, two songs by Mr. Damrosch and M. Tchaikovsky, and the Prelude and Flower Maidens' scene from Wagner's "Parsifal."

New York Times, May 10, 1891
The Music Hall concerts

. . . Then came the star of the concert, Tchaikovsky, with his B-flat minor piano Concerto in which Miss Aus der Ohe played the solo part, while the composer conducted. The performance of this melodious and characteristic work, in which there are some of Tchaikovsky's most popular ideas, was generally good. The wood wind, which had done so well in the symphony, went to pieces once or twice in this work, and Miss Aus der Ohe's playing, while technically crisp and smooth (except in one or two passages where a few notes were dropped) was strangely deficient in solidity and richness of tone. The composer conducted admirably and the splendid verve of the concluding passage evoked great enthusiasm. Tchaikovsky and the pianist were recalled half a dozen times, Miss Aus der Ohe showing the most charming modesty and tact in her refusal to accept any of the applause for herself.

The Press, May 10, 1891
Close of the Music Festival

The number of principal interest at the afternoon concert was Tchaikovsky's piano concerto in B-flat minor, op. 23, which was played by Miss Adele Aus der Ohe, the composer leading the Symphony orchestra. Under his inspiring beat the band played this beautiful composition with spirit and feeling, and Miss Aus der Ohe also surpassed some of her previous achievements, giving a brilliant reading to the piano part. The audience which again taxed the utmost capacity of the hall, was very enthusiastic, recalling the conductor and Miss Aus der Ohe again and again amid tumultous cheerings. . . .

DIARY   May 10

It's been a very difficult and heavy day. In the morning I was harried by visitors. Who has not come? Suave, interesting Mr. Korbay; a young, very handsome composer, Klein; von Sachs; the pianist friend with gold in her teeth; Mr. Suro with his beautiful wife, a doctor of laws; and I don't know who else. I was simply driven into unconsciousness. At 1 o'clock came out to visit the nihilist Stark-Stoleshnikov, but he lives at such a distance and the heat was so awful,— that I had to postpone it. Dropped in at Hoffman's and there met Mr. Parris, a ship companion,—the one who provided me with cigarettes. He hates America and thinks only of leaving. From there hurried for lunch at Dr. Neftel's. Was barely in time. Dr. Neftel turned out to be a Russian or at least was brought up in Russia. His wife, as I finally found out, is a Georgian princess, a cousin of Egor Ivanovich. They have lived in America since 1860. They often go to Europe, but have not been in Russia since then. Why do they avoid it—it was embarrassing to inquire. Both are fierce patriots, and love Russia with a genuine love. I took more liking to the husband than to the wife. There was something gentle, kind, nice, and sincere to be felt in each Russian word pronounced (not without difficulty) and in each idle motion made by this weary and somewhat sorrowful old man. Concerning Russia he spoke always of how despotism and bureaucratic administration prevent it from standing at the head of mankind. He repeated that idea with other variations countless times. His wife is a type of breezy Moscow mistress. Wants to look clever and independent but overall, it seems, she has neither intellect nor independence. Both love music very much and know it well. Once Neftel became famous for something in the field of medicine and is very much respected in New York. I think that he is a freethinker, who once drew the wrath of government upon himself and opportunely escaped from Russia; but apparently his present-day liberalism is far from nihilism and anarchism. Both repeated several times that they don't hob-nob with local nihilists. After breakfast at their place (about 3'clock) ran (for lack of cabmen one has to run all the time) to V. N. MacGahan. If one could say that the Neftels live luxuriously, the surroundings of this correspondent for Russian newspapers and magazines are quite like a student's. She lives in a boarding room, that is, in a clean, furnished house, where all share a common parlor and a common dining room downstairs, and have living quarters on the upper floors. In her place I found a very strange young Russian man named Griboedov, who spoke in broken Russian but perfect French and English. He has the appearance of modern dandy and slightly puts on airs. Later the well-known sculptor Kamensky appeared, who has lived in America twenty years already (I don't know why). He is an old man, with a deep scar on his forehead, ailing, and quite lamentable to see. He startled me by asking me to tell all that I know of present-day Russia. I was quite lost before that formidable task, but, fortunately, Varvara Nikolaevna began to talk of my musical affairs and then I glanced at my watch and saw that it was time to run home and change for the dinner at Carnegie's. On Sundays all the cafes are closed. Since they are the only places where one can: 1) buy cigarettes, and 2) fulfill a certain need of nature, and I was in extreme need of both, one can just imagine how great were my sufferings until at last I ran home. Traces of English Puritanism, revealed in such absurd trifles as, for instance, the fact that it's impossible to get a shot of whiskey or a glass of beer on Sundays other than by fraud, are quite revolting to me. People say that the legislators who issued this law in New York State are themselves awful drunkards. Barely managed to change and then went to Carnegie in a carriage (which I had to call specially and pay dearly for). Overall, this ultra-rich man lives no more luxuriously than others. Dining with us were the Renos, the Damroschs, the architect of the Music Hall with his wife, an unknown gentleman, and a fat ladyfriend of Mrs. Damrosch. I again sat next to this very aristocratic lady, so graceful in her air. Carnegie, this remarkable original who rose from telegraph boy to become in the course of years one of American's foremost men of wealth, but remained a modest and simple man, never one to turn his nose up—inspires in me unusual warm feelings, probably because he is also filled with kindly feelings for me. During the whole evening, he showed his love to me in an extraordinarily peculiar way. He clasped my hands, shouting that I am the uncrowned but still genuine king of music; embraced me (without kissing—men never kiss here); he stood on tiptoe and raised his hands up high to express my greatness; and finally threw all the company in delight by imitating my conducting. He did this so seriously, so well, and so accurately, that I myself was enraptured. His wife, an extremely simple and pretty young lady, also showed her sympathy for me in every way. All this was pleasing and somehow embarrassing at the same time. I was very glad to depart for home at 11 o'clock. Reno walked me home. I packed for the tomorrow's trip.

DAY SIXTEENTH   New York—Niagara

Evening Post, May 11, 1891
End of the Music Festival

The Music Festival came to the close with two concerts on Saturday, both of which were well attended. The most important number in the afternoon was Tchaikovsky's first piano concerto which was conducted by the composer and played by Miss Aus der Ohe in such a way, that the audience recalled them no less then six times at the end. Beethoven's Fifth Symphony, which opened the afternoon concert, was badly played, while the final piece, the Flower Maiden chorus from "Parsifal," was well sung. The performance of "Israel in Egypt" in the evening was interesting to the English-minded, who ask for little but sonority and religion in an oratorio, while others would have been more gratified if there had been more shading in the choruses, which make up the greater part of the work.

The Music Festival of 1891 will be chiefly remembered as the occasion of the opening of the finest music-hall in America, if not in the world, and for the first appearance in America of Mr. Tchaikovsky. Apart from these two factors, the six concerts given last week hardly deserved the title of festival concerts, as the forces employed and the programmes did not differ materially from ordinary programmes. Had it not been for the new Music Hall and the Russian composer, New Yorkers would not perhaps have taken much interest in the festival, as they have more music than they can digest during the regular season; under the given circumstances, however, a festival was perfectly justifiable, and it was easy to predict that it would be a financial success. For some time the new hall will continue to attract the curious, and after that all concerts given there will have to stand on their own merits.

The engagement of Mr. Tchaikovsky is in itself a significant fact, as it is perhaps the first time that an invitation has been sent from this country to a musician who is a composer only, and not a virtuoso (except at the conductor's desk). If this should signalize the opening of a new era, when the general public will begin to realize that a creative artist is of infinitely more importance than a mere interpreter—singer or player—something will have been gained apart from the pleasure afforded by the performance of five of Mr. Tchaikovsky's compositions under his direction, which insured correctness in all things, and especially in the most important of all factors—that of tempo.

The extraordinary enthusiasm with which Mr. Tchaikovsky was received at each appearance, and the way in which he monopolised the interest in the festival, bore witness to the wisdom of our counsel when we advised the directors of the Metropolitan Opera-House, a few months ago, to retain German opera, but to supplement it by the importation of some famous French or Russian composer to bring out the best of his own operas. Gounod, Saint-Saens, Massenet, Tchaikovsky, would have been available, and perhaps even Rubinstein, for though he has refused to come as pianist, it would be much easier to induce him to come as composer and conductor. As for Mr. Tchaikovsky, he has written no less than nine operas and ballets, several of which could, no doubt, have been produced with success at the Metropolitan under his own direction. . . .

PETER TCHAIKOVSKY TO MODEST TCHAIKOVSKY

New York, May 11, 1891

Modia,

Just received your letter of the 26th. Where did you get the idea that I've grown cold to *Iolantha?* It is because I am in love with her more than ever, that I postponed work until next year. I desire and I can make a *chef d'oeuvre* from it, but I must not be in a hurry to do so. Ask yourself, when would I have found time to do it properly??? The tension would have overcome my strength, and as a result it would have been a hasty, mediocre composition.

Now am going to Niagara. No time to write. I kiss and embrace you.

P. Tchaikovsky

DIARY   May 11

Mayer called for me at 8:15. What indeed would I have done without Mayer? How would I have gotten myself a ticket of the exact kind that's required; how would I have approached the railroad; how would I have found out at which hours, how, and what I have to do? I boarded the car-salon. This is like our armchaired car, except that the armchairs are set closer together and against the windows, but in such a way that it's possible to spin around. The windows are big and the view on both sides is entirely open. Next to this car was the car-restaurant, and several cars further was the smoking car with a buffet. The traffic from car to car is absolutely free and much more comfortable than with us, for the passages are covered. The servants, that is, the conductors, the waiters in the car-restaurant, and at the buffet of the smoking compartment, are Negroes; all very obliging and polite. At 12 o'clock I had breakfast (the price of the breakfast is one dollar) by menu, entitling me to eat as much as I want of dishes featured in menu. Dined at 6, again choosing from among several dozen dishes anything I wanted and in whatever amount— all for one dollar. The cars are far more luxurious than ours, despite the absence of classes. The luxury is actually quite superfluous, e.g., the frescoes, the crystal decorations, etc. There are numerous toilets, that is, sections with washing-sets, with installed cold and hot water, towels (there is, in general, amazing plentifulness regarding towels here), cakes of soap, brushes, etc. One can roam about on the train and wash as much as one wants. There is a bath and a barber's shop. All this is convenient and comfortable—and yet our cars are more attractive to me for some reason. But probably this is the aftermath of my homesickness, which oppressed and gnawed at me again yesterday, all day long to the point of madness.

PETER TCHAIKOVSKY TO MODEST TCHAIKOVSKY

Utica, May 11, 1891

I had no time to write you this morning, to tell you that you misunderstood my letters from Rouen to you and Vsevolozhsky. More than ever I am fond of the plot of *Iolanthe*

and your libretto is quite well done. But while I was in
Rouen illustrating gingerbread, soldiers, dolls, etc. with music, I saw that I had much work yet on the ballet and that
only thereafter could I start on the opera. I also realized
that neither on the way to America, nor in America, nor
even on the way back would I be able to work. These
things brought me to despair as I felt the full impossibility
of my properly fulfilling the accepted task. Then I stopped
loving *Iolanthe*, and only because I wished to love it once
again and passionately did I decide to give it up. Once I
gave it up—I became fond of it. Oh yes, I will write the
kind of opera to make everyone cry,—but only for the season of 1892–93.

Am writing this letter in the buffet-car, the sole place
where smoking is allowed. Also there are furnished desks
here for writing letters and telegrams. The train is going at
an unusual speed, and it's difficult to write. The amenities
and comforts of American trains are amazing, but ours are
better in many respects. No stops at all. One sits, sits, and
gets tired of sitting. However I will provide details in my
diary. I ate my lunch in the dining car. It was long and
hearty but bad as meals usually are here.

I embrace you. Tonight at 10 p.m. I will be in Niagara.

DIARY   May 11 (continued)

At 8:30 o'clock we arrived in Buffalo. Here two gentlemen were waiting for me, whom Mayer had asked to see
me off one train and onto another. It is indeed quite difficult to find the right track in this labyrinthine junction of
various railways lines. One of the men was a Polish pianist.
The rendezvous with these gentlemen lasted only 10 minutes. In 50 minutes after leaving Buffalo, I was already in
Niagara Falls. Was booked at the Hotel Kaltenbach, where
accommodations were prepared, again through Mayer. The
hotel is modest, in the style of small Swiss ones,—but very
clean and, most importantly, quite suitable to me, since

everyone speaks German here. Drank tea, unfortunately
with some gentleman who annoyed me with talk. Felt unusually tired, I think, because the air in the train was terribly stuffy. Americans, especially women, are afraid of
draughts, in consequence of which, the windows are closed
all the time and outside air is not permitted to circulate.
And then you have to sit longer than we do. Hardly any
stops at all. It was especially tiresome, since only the first
hours of the trip, on the bank of Hudson River, were interesting for the eye; during all the remaining time the region
was flat and scarcely attractive. I retired early. The noise of
waterfalls in the night's silence is quite audible.

DAY SEVENTEENTH

DIARY   May 12, Niagara

   Rose about 8 o'clock. Breakfast at 8. Made the acquaintance of the owner, Mr. Kaltenbach. A slightly reserved but
quite courteous and distinguished German. A landau was
already waiting. There are no guides here—and that's fine!
A coachman drives one wherever, to all the proper places,
and, partly by words, partly by gestures shows those who
don't speak English, what to do. At first we headed for
"Goat Island" across the old bridge. There, making a right,
we stopped, and the coachman told me to come down to
the level of the "American Falls." I will not describe the
beauty of the waterfall, for these things are too difficult for
words. The beauty and majesty of the spectacle are really
amazing. Having walked about and viewed this part of the
falls for a good while—basically, the falls split into several
separate waterfalls, two of which are colossal (especially the
second)—we set off along the shore of the island for Three
Sisters Island. The whole tour is charming, particularly at
this time of the year. The greenery is entirely fresh and in
the grass, my darlings, the dandelions, are showing off. I

badly wanted to pick a few of these yellow beauties with the
scent of freshness and spring, but at every step stands a
sign with the warning that even "wild flowers" can't be
picked. Then I viewed the main waterfall, the "Horseshoe
Falls." A grandiose picture. From there we returned to the
mainland and crossed the marvelous, audacious, wonderful
bridge to the Canadian side. This bridge was built, or better to say, thrown across the Niagara, only two years ago.
One's head swims when looking down. On the Canadian
side I made myself venture onward in order not to be tormented by the thought that I was afraid. Wearing a very
ugly change of clothes, I descended in an elevator under
the falls, walked through a tunnel, and at last stood under
the very falls, which was interesting but a little frightening.
From above I was pestered to buy photographs and various
kinds of rubbish. The importunity and impudence of these
leeches would have been incomprehensible, had I not discovered from the features of the men and women, preying
upon me with offers of favour, that they were Jews. Besides, Canada is no longer America. From there we went
downstream to the "Rapid's View." The Niagara, a river
wider than the Volga, divides into arms, falls down enormous cliffs, and here suddenly narrows to the width of the
Seine. Then as if having stored up its power, it stumbles
onto the rapids and enters into battle with them. Thence by
the funicular railroad I descended with a boy guide and
walked a while on the bank, on level with the raging river.
The view reminds me of Imatra, but in greater dimensions.
Then I walked a while more, got in my landau again near
the bridge, and came home shortly before dinner. In the
Table d'hotel I sat at a distance from others. The dinner
was European and very delicious. After dinner walked to
the waterfalls and generally around the city. During this
stroll, just as in the morning, I could not overcome a particular, no doubt nervous, tiredness, which prevented me
from duly enjoying the walk and the beauty of the vicinity.
It's as if something inside me came to pieces and the ma-
chine now functions less smoothly. At 6:15 o'clock I de-

parted in a sleeping car, in a private room. The Negro servant is muddle-headed and not especially polite. On his account I couldn't get any food and went to sleep hungry. There are all possible amenities: washstand, soap, towels, and a luxurious bed. Still I slept badly.

DAY EIGHTEENTH

Musical Courier [Weekly Magazine], May 13, 1891
The music at the Festival—Tuesday evening, May 5

The Beethoven overture Leonore No. 3 received a very loose, ragged reading. Everybody, including Mr. Damrosch, was evidently too much excited to play smoothly, but when Mr. Peter Tchaikovsky took the band in hand all was changed. The great Russian's beat is firm, forcible, even a little harsh, but as to its effectiveness there can be no doubt, for the orchestra followed him implicitly and not he the orchestra.

Comparisons could never be more odious than between Walter Damrosch and Tchaikovsky, but that they were made that night goes without saying. All the personal magnetism and virility the younger conductor lacks were gratifyingly present in the conducting of the great composer, and though his "Marche Solennelle" in D is a bit of musical claptrap, redolent of Meyerbeer and Wagner, and not a good imitation of either, still the audience fairly shouted at its composer, and he had to bow his acknowledgements four or five times. In point of strict fact, from the time that Tchaikovsky made his initial bend of the back until he, with Adele Aus der Ohe, smiled his farewell at a New York audience, the festival was emphatically a Tchaikovsky one.

Without his presence it languished and it would have been a wise thing if the management had allowed him to conduct some of the overture fantasies. It was probably unjust, even absurd, to bring a man 4000 miles to conduct a march, a suite, short choruses and a piano concerto.

If the May festival had been downright and honest in its intentions it would have resolved itself into a Tchaikovsky celebration instead of digging up a lot of old musical bones for the greater edification of Mr. Damrosch and the Oratorio Society.

And what could be more appropriate? That Tchaikovsky is one of the greatest composers alive will not be gainsaid and his presence in our midst was an honor and a delight not often vouchsafed us. . . .

Thursday afternoon, May 7

The afternoon was literally made radiant by the personality of Tchaikovsky, which was overwhelming. He conducted his superbly wrought and richly colored third orchestral suite, with which he has had such success throughout Europe.

It contains in a crystallized form all of its composer's genius. It has been heard in New York before under Mr. Thomas' baton. Its elegiac character at the outset deepens at the end into one of the most striking and brilliant climaxes imaginable. The scherzo is in rhythms and themes thoroughly national. The variations are forceful and display that marvellous handling of orchestral material and cunning development of an Idea that place Tchaikovsky in the foremost rank of living composers.

With the exception of Brahms he has no peer as a variation writer.

The brilliant "Polacca" which closed the movement received a fiery reading and pandemonium reigned, for the large audience insisted on the composer receiving their plaudits until he was almost exhausted. Nobody appeared more delighted at Tchaikovsky than Walter Damrosch, who led the applause. . . .

Saturday, afternoon, May 9

. . . Tchaikovsky again demonstrated the warm interest he has aroused, for he was saluted royally by a very large and overheated audience. (The hall is not a cool one, despite its size.)

The concerto, which we have heard from Mr. Rummel and Mr. Joseffy, went very smoothly—too smoothly, in fact, for its dramatic force and almost barbaric fire and fury. Miss Adele Aus der Ohe is altogether too ladylike in her style to interpret Mr. Tchaikovsky's passion-laden phrases.

She played in a prim, neat fashion, that utterly killed the fragrance of the delicate scherzo with its valse-like rhythm.

The work was eminently better interpreted by Helen Hopekirk with the Nikisch band in Boston.

Mr. Tchaikovsky conducted in his usual vigorous fashion and with the pianist was recalled many times. . . .

The raconteur

All Jimmie's horses and Carnegie's men
Can only Walter make
Conductor "pro tem."

I was forcibly reminded of this Humpty Dumpty-like paraphrase all last week, for, with all Blaine's political and social influence and Andrew Carnegie's financial prestige, Walter Damrosch appeared to be very little more than a figurehead last week at the May Music Festival. But a modest, amiable figurehead I admit. Tchaikovsky—what a delightful surprise he was to all of us!

The personality of composers is not always a pleasant one, but in Peter Tchaikovsky one finds a cultured man of the world, excessively modest and retiring.

We have entertained a musical god during the past week and I fear me greatly that many of us were not aware of the fact.

I bethought me, as I looked on his earnest face, heavy brow, with its condensed look about the eyes, that there stood a man who might be called the greatest in the country.

Do you notice I don't say the greatest musician but the greatest man?

Let me see; of individualities living among us we still have dear old Walt Whitman, who represents a primal force, but in the best of whose work, despite its rugged sincerity, there is always an unfinished quantity.

James Russell Lowell is still alive, so is gentle Oliver Wendell Holmes. Howells writes novels, Jim Blaine is a mighty force in politics and Bob Ingersoll is a remarkable personality. We have a few strong painters, fewer sculptors, our poets are mainly imitative or echoes; in a word, where in art, music, literature, politics, religion, is just such a forceful, fiery, magnetic man such as Peter Tchaikovsky?

You can't name him.

This man epitomizes young Russia in his music, he preaches more treason in his music than Alexander Pushkin ever uttered. He is not as profound as Brahms, but he is more poetic.

Above all he paints better than the Hamburg composer.

His brush is dipped into more glowing colors, his palette contains more hues and the barbaric swing of his work is tempered by European culture and restraint.

Take the piano concertos in B-flat minor and G minor. They are about as unorthodox as we can well imagine.

I like the second the better, but in neither of them do I find real writing for the instrument. Tchaikovsky thinks orchestrally, and if the idea does not suit the keyboard—well, all the worse for the keyboard. There was a story afloat that Nicholas Rubinstein helped him to fix up the piano part of the two concertos.

From Tchaikovsky I indirectly got at the true story.

When Peter (Pete, to be a little familiar—I don't like his middle name at all, do you?) had finished the first work he showed it to Nick Rubinstein, whom he pronounced to have been a better pianist than his brother Tony. They all lived in the same house in Moscow, Rafael Joseffy occupying the top floor, and he says that whenever he wanted to practice Tchaikovsky always wanted to sleep, so that trouble ensued daily.

Well, Rubinstein looked through the concerto and dismissed it disdainfully. "Unklaviermassig [unpianolike], mein lieber Tschike." (He called him Tschike for short, and that reminds me that all rumors that are current about his inability to pronounce his own name were set at rest last week by the publication in the Novgorod "Bi-Daily" of an article on the "use and abuse of the letter "j" in Russian proper names." Mr. Tchaikovsky is a member of the Moscow Philological Society, admission to which august body depends on the applicant's ability to pronounce his own name. It goes without saying that these learned men can carelessly remark "Prejavolowski" at any hour of the day.)

Tchaikovsky bided his time and gave the work to Von Bulow, after erasing Rubinstein's name on the dedication and substituting that of Von Bulow. Rubinstein suddenly discovered the merits of the work and to him Tchaikovsky dedicated the second concerto in G.

The brilliancy and daring of the great Russian are particularly well illustrated in his third suite, with its national coloring and complex rhythms. I like the fifth symphony better, and I am sorry he didn't conduct it while he was here.

Tchaikovsky sometimes says great things in a great manner, and that is why I think he is the greatest man in the country at present, for we have many men saying things which are not great, nor are they said greatly.

The figure of Tchaikovsky looms grandly over these petty personalities as a poetic, intense thinker, who in an age of self gain and grasping greed looks afar, as from a peak, and sees beautiful things, which he repeats to us afterward in his music. I like, I admire, I even reverence, his kindly love of his fellow men which throbs through his scores.

He has suffered much. No man could pen that wonderful "Nur wer die Sehnsucht kennt," which interprets Goethe's idea better than Goethe himself, without having tasted at the acid spring of sorrow. He has loved, else his "Romeo and

Juliet" overture is a farce and a make believe, and the passionate heart beats it causes in you are lies, too.

That were hard to believe.

He knows his Hamlet, he knows his counterpoint, and,
above all, he knows himself.

He has the Calmuck in him, and it breaks out, but is soon
subdued, for his reason rules his temperament.

He is a strong man.

He says great things in a great manner, and that is why I
call him the greatest man at present in this broad and fair
land.

For the rest, he is a pleasant appearing gentleman who per-
spires audibly and puts his pocket handkerchief in his left
hand trousers pocket (Moscow etiquette I am told) and always looks for it during a fermata.

I was amused at John Rietzel in the orchestra after the suite
was finished. He stood up and in the most significant manner touched his forehead and pointed to Pete, who was bow-
ing his acknowledgements, as one should say "a great head."
Right you are, Mr. Rietzel, a great head indeed!

DIARY   May 13

Awoke at 5 o'clock, tired and full of trying thoughts of
the coming terrible week. Came to my place at 8 o'clock.
Took a bath, was glad to see good Max, but was distressed
with reading in the newspaper information about the attempted assassination on the Heir.[36] I am also taking to
heart that there are no letters from home,—I expected
them in a great number. Visitors: Reinhard, Mowson,
Smith, Huss, etc. In view of the remoteness of the different
parts of New York, in which I had to be today, I hired a
private carriage. First of all I went to say farewell to Damrosch, who is starting for Europe. He asked me to take him
on as an apprentice. I refused, of course, but unwillingly
revealed my horror too much over the thought of Dam-

rosch's arriving at my place in the village, intent upon studying!!! From there hurried to Reno's for lunch. The coachman was quite drunk, and completely failed to understand where I had to be driven. It's well that I am now already capable of orienting myself in New York. As usual, the Reno family displayed much cordiality. From there to Mayer's, where I had to make the acquaintance of Mr. Keidel, the partner of Knabe. So it went. Then, still with the same drunk coachman, Mayer and I made haste to reach the huge ferryboat, which conveys carriages with horses, and people across the East River, and from there to his *dacha* [Russ., country cottage used especially in summer] by train. Felt so fatigued, exasperated, and unhappy that I could hardly refrain from tears. The Mayer's dacha and the others in that vicinity are very much in the style of the dachas near Moscow. The only difference is that near Moscow there are groves, grass, and flowers; there is nothing here except sand. Nothing drearier than these houses could be imagined, were it not for the ocean, which compels one to forget everything that is associated with the charms of summer or country life in our minds. Shortly after our arrival we sat down to dine. The younger son of Mayer, that true German, is a boy of fourteen, who is so Americanized that he speaks German like this: "Du haben kalt in Russland?" The family are kind and nice but their intellectual level is very low, in consequence of which I was fiercely bored and felt burdened. After dinner we walked in the sand by the ocean itself, which seethed a little. The air is fresh and clear here and this stroll gave me pleasure and relief. Spent the night at their place, and slept badly.

DAY NINETEENTH

DIARY   May 14

Got up about 6 o'clock. Walked to the sea and admired it. After breakfast we went to the city. Craved at least a bit

to be alone,—but it was difficult. Miss Ivy Ross appeared.
My letter about Wagner, sent to her, was published, and
made a sensation. Mr. Anton Seidl, the famous Wagnerian
conductor, answered it at length in, what seemed to me, a
very gentlemanly tone.

Morning Journal, May 10, 1891
A Defence of Wagner by Anton Seidl—the noted musician
and orchestral leader

You ask me whether I read Tchaikovsky's article on Wagner
in last Sunday's JOURNAL. Why, to be sure, I have read it!
Who has not read it? And who, in New York, was more astonished than I? It is enough to create surprise to find a man
asserting that Wagner would have created better works of
the symphonic order if he had chosen to compose such, than
operas.

Up to the present day, we poor mortals have considered it
indisputable that Wagner, as a composer of opera, caused a
reformation, or a revolution, or whatever you may choose to
call it: and that, according to the taste and the conception
(understanding) of our times Wagner's operas or musical
dramas have reached the highest point ever attained.

And now Tchaikovsky undertakes to say that Wagner followed a wrong path: that he should have written works of a
symphonic character. This is something quite new and an
opinion which I, in common with thousands of other people,
shall not subscribe to. I even incline to the belief that Tchaikovsky himself treats the orchestral part in a symphonic
manner in his opera "Pique Dame," "Onegin," etc.

And then what is the meaning of the term "symphonic
treatment?" If it be to work in thematical or polyphonic
manner or after a certain "leit-motiv," then I may well say
that nowadays everybody composes in the same fashion, and
any one who avoids this goes down and is never heard of
again.

All the arguments Tchaikovsky brings forward as examples of symphonic treatment are founded on the very nature of the thing itself.

If the action demands that the rustling of forest leaves should be expressed in music, we have to do it. It is only his own talent that enabled Wagner to portray this rustling of forest leaves better than Franchetti, or that caused his grand funeral march to be superior to Donizetti's "Sebastian" or Reimecke's "Zur Trauerfeier" or any one else's save Beethoven. Verily, all civilized nations rejoice that, beside this "Waldweben" and the funeral march in "Siegfried" and in "Goetterdaemmerung," we find pages as grand and as beautiful as these.

I am firmly convinced that Tchaikovsky himself follows the path indicated above. This is shown in his wonderful Suite No. 3, which he rendered in such a masterly manner the other day in the Music Hall. He proved himself a great symphonist, but at the same time a good composer of opera, as, when the suite was nearing its end, one could almost see a grand festival on the stage.

Now I should like to say a few words about the so-called "Wagner cult." Much has been written lately about the "Wagner craze," the burning of incense at Wagner's shrine, about how Wagner is over-estimated, concerning the intolerance of Wagnerites and their delusion that he is the only great one, etc. All this belongs in the realm of imagination, not to use a stronger expression. Of whom do these critics speak? Of Richter, Levi, Mottl, Sucher, Weingartner, Strauss, Nikisch, Pauer, Mahler, Fischer, Schuch and all the others? Is it not true that the very men just enumerated have built the roads for the entrance into the concert and upon the stage of Brahms, Berlioz, Cornelius, Dvorak, Tchaikovsky, Chabrier, Rubinstein, etc.? Haven't they opened their programmes for classical music in a way never known before?

Wagner himself was an enthusiastic admirer of all the classic composers, as his glowing words of praise witnessed. Has he not built on foundations Weber, Mozart and Beethoven

laid? Is there anything grander than his essay on Beethoven?
Is it possible to speak with more enthusiasm than he did of
Mozart?

Where is intolerance? Presumably only in heads of a few
conceited ignoramuses! There are no Wagnerites that are
not also followers of Beethoven, Bach and Mozart. He who
would deny this cannot be classified among the followers of
Wagner. Any one who understands Wagner understands
Beethoven or Bach also.

Viewed from a musical standpoint, there are only two classes
of people: those who understand music and those who do
not. It is but natural that every one should have his favorite
composer, just as he has his favorite author or painter, whose
ideas and feelings he believes to be akin to his own.

But no honest musician would idolize one composer and
condemn all the rest. Some people endeavor to make it appear that I myself have a weakness in this respect, but I would
declare once for all that this is wrong.

If there was too much Wagner in the Metropolitan Opera
House, it was not my fault at all, but Wagner's, as he had
composed those operas the New York public liked best. I
have always been in favor of putting new compositions of
Massenet, Chabrier, Reyer, Verdi, Mascagni, Lalo, Berlioz,
Liszt and others before the public.

The responsibility for not heeding these recommendations
rests not with me. It costs money to bring out new compositions, and where no money is forthcoming one cannot do it.
Under these circumstances the directors fell back on Wagner, who always filled the house, and that without great ex-
pense. All this the New York public has seen. Heaven grant
that it may see some new compositions next season!

DIARY   May 14 (continued)

She [Ivy Ross] came to ask that I answer Seidl's letter.
I nearly started to write the reply,—but Mr. Ditman

appeared and stayed unusually long, relating very uninteresting and hundred-times-heard local musical gossip. Then
there was a correspondent of a Philadelphian newspaper—
apparently, an especially sincere admirer of mine. I had to
speak English; I made progress; spoke certain things quite
well. Wrote letters.

PETER TCHAIKOVSKY TO VLADIMIR DAVIDOV

New York, May 14, 1891

It has now reached the point that I am definitely unable
to write letters. Not a minute is free. I scarcely find time to
write my diary. I made a trip to Niagara. I'd barely returned, when I had to go off again to a certain Mr. Mayer's
dacha; the few hours before that I devoted to visits, then
was invited out to breakfast and had to face the usual fuss.

Am unconscionably tired. Today I must attend a big dinner and depart for Baltimore at midnight; tomorrow a rehearsal and concert; on the day after, Washington, then
Philadelphia, then two days here (all my time is taken already), and, at last, on the morning of the 21st, my departure. Lord! Will I at last be awaiting this much-desired minute?!!

About one week after you receive this letter, I'll see you!!
This seems to me an unattainable, fabulous happiness; I try
somewhat less to think of that in order to have the strength
to bear these few, tedious, final days. And yet I foresee that
I will recall America with love. They have truly given me a
fine welcome here.

Am sending several newspaper clippings. I will bring
with me many others. I think that it will be more interesting for all of you to read my diary instead of fragmentary
news in the letters.

I embrace you all.

In a week!!!

P. Tchaikovsky

   I had breakfast downstairs alone at the hotel, took a walk
through Central Park. According to my promise, called on
Mayer to write the reference for Knabe pianos. This is at
last the clue to Mayer's wooing!!! All those gifts, all that
spending of Knabe's money on my behalf, all that inconceivable attentiveness, was just the price for future advertisement!!![37] I asked Mayer to compose the requested reference himself; he sat long but for some reason could not
contrive of anything and asked to postpone the matter until
the next meeting. After that, I paid a visit to Mr. Tretbar,
the representative of Steinway, who, having been notified
by Jurgenson, had until now been awaiting me with a letter
from Peter Ivanovich, having no desire to come to me first.
I deliberately postponed the visit to this meticulous German
till such time, that we would have no chance to become
closer acquainted. Packed at home. Soon Reinhard appeared with a letter from Mayer in which the latter asked
me to sign the reference for Knabe pianos. In this draft of
the reference I was said that I found Knabe pianos indis-
putably the best in America. Since in actuality I not only do
not find them so, but recognize Steinway (regardless of
comparative impoliteness of its representative, Tretbar,
concerning me) to be undoubtedly superior, I rejected this
wording of my reference-advertisement. I entrusted Reinhard to tell Mayer that for all my gratitude, I don't wish to
tell a lie. Then came the *Herald*'s reporter, a very appealing
man. Thomas Junior at last appeared, with whom I headed
in the Hyde's carriage to the latter. It's regrettable that I
definitely can't afford to describe all the fascination, attrac-
tiveness, originality of this couple. Hyde greeted me with
the words: "Kak washe zdaroyue, sidite pozhaliust." [Bro-
ken Russian: "How do you feel? Sit down, please."] With
that he began to roar like a madman. Then his wife roared
and I roared and Thomas, too. It turns out that he had
bought a Russian self-instruction manual and learned by

heart several phrases in order to surprise me. Mrs. Hyde insisted that I take a moment to smoke a cigarette in her parlor—the utmost hospitality for an American lady. After the cigarette we went to dine. The table was densely covered with flowers; each of us had a little bouquet for his holder. Then Hyde quite unexpectedly became serious and, lowering his eyes, said the Pater Noster. I did as the others, i.e., lowered my eyes, too. Then began an endlessly long dinner, with vast pretension (for instance, everyone was served ice cream in the form of an enormous, lifelike rose, from the middle of which the ice cream fell out). In the midst of dinner Mrs. Hyde pressed me to smoke. All this lasted very, very long, so that I was tired and almost totally lethargic, especially since all the time I had to speak English or hear out the unsuccessful attempts of both hosts to say something in French. At 10 o'clock I departed with Thomas. At home Reinhard was awaiting me. We drank some beer downstairs and started with my suitcases for Downtown by the elevated; there we crossed the Hudson on a ferry boat and at last approached the railroad station. Here Reinhard (without whose help I would have been lost) settled me into a comfortable compartment; a gentle Negro made my bed, on which I dropped dressed, since I had no strength to undress; I soon fell dead asleep. Slept soundly but little. The Negro awoke me one hour before the train arrived in Baltimore.

DAY TWENTIETH

DIARY   May 15

In the hotel was received as usual with coldness and neglect. Finding myself alone in my room, I felt unusually miserable and unhappy, mostly because nobody speaks anything but English. Slept a bit. Set out for the restaurant to eat breakfast and was irritated very much by the Negro servant, who failed to understand that I simply wanted tea with bread and butter. I had to go to the office, where no one understood anything either. Finally some gentleman who spoke German came to my aid. As soon as I sat down, stout Knabe arrived, and soon I saw Adele Aus der Ohe with her sister and was terribly glad for it; at least we in music are not strange people. With them started in a carriage for the rehearsal. This latter was held on the stage of the Lyceum. The orchestra appeared to be small (only 4 first violins played!!!) but rather good. There was no point in considering the Third Suite. Instead we decided to play the "Serenade for Strings," which the musicians didn't know at all, for Mr. Herbert, the conductor, hadn't even bothered to play through it in advance, as Reno had promised me. The concerto with Aus der Ohe again went well, but the "Serenade" required a good bit of time. The musicians were impatient, and the young concertmaster was not even especially polite, for he rather too strongly conveyed the feeling that it was time to quit. True, this unhappy traveling orchestra is much fatigued by its trips. After the rehearsal headed for home again with Aus der Ohe, changed in half an hour, and went at once to the concert. As usual for a matinee, I conducted in a frock-coat. Everything went quite well but I didn't sense any special delight in the audience, at least in comparison with New York. After the concert we went home to change and not half an hour had passed before Knabe, that man so colossal in figure and hospitality, came for us. This beardless giant held a feast in my honour at his place. I found a big company there: Mlle. von Fernow (a former friend of Kotek), who came to Baltimore as a music teacher; the composer and the director of the Conservatory, Hamerick; the very old Courlaender, a pianist; Burmeister, the composer; Fincke, professor of singing and a very witty and eloquent table speaker; two sons of Knabe; his two nephews; the music critic of the *Sun* (the local newspaper); and a few more gentlemen, whose names I don't recall, one of whom had been to Petersburg.

The latter amused us with tricks after dinner. The dinner was endless, terribly delicious, with an abundance of food and wine to which Knabe zealously added throughout the course of the dinner. Beginning in the middle of the dinner I felt an unusual fatigue and an unimaginable hatred against everyone and mostly against two my neighbors: Mlle. v. Fernow and the sister of Aus der Ohe. After dinner I conversed a bit with everyone—most of all with old Courlaender, watched the tricks of the same gentleman; listened to the piano concerto of the young composer, Burmeister, and smoked and drank without end. At 11:30 Knabe drove the Aus der Ohe sisters and me home. I slumped down on my bed like a sheaf [of wheat] and at once fell dead asleep.

DAY TWENTY-FIRST

The Sun, Baltimore, May 16, 1891
Great Tchaikovsky

A small part of musical Baltimore wended its way in the rain Tchaikovskyward yesterday afternoon and enjoyed one of the greatest treats that have been given to musicloving people this season. The audience at the Lyceum was not large, but it was a good audience for all that—good in that it knew how to appreciate to its utmost the worth of what was given, and good also in knowing how to make a big noise to show its enthusiasm. Many of the most prominent of Baltimore musicians were present, and the great composer was welcomed in a way that must have satisfied even one so accustomed to plaudits.

Only two works on the long programme brought out Tchaikovsky both as composer and conductor. The first was the B-flat minor Piano Concerto and the second a suite for string orchestra, both of intense interest, full of the fire and dash of the Russian, the finish and scholarly workmanship

of the master and the intelligence and refinement of the artist musician. The suite was a delightful combination of dance
rhythms, each movement bringing out melodious subjects and
rich harmonic treatments. But it was the concerto, led by
Tchaikovsky and played by Adele Aus der Ohe, that made
the concert so enjoyable.

Tchaikovsky and Aus der Ohe. What a combination; the
one leading his splendid work with force and understanding
that inspired the musicians, the other bringing to the piano
all the life of her musician's personality, and expressing it
through rare technical skill. When the concerto was over the
air rang with applause, and composer and player were recalled again and again to the stage, until applause broke into
cheers. Tchaikovsky taking his honors quietly and modestly
and making repeated efforts to keep himself in the background, and Aus der Ohe just as persistently drawing him
to the front to share the praise with her.

The orchestra, composed of well-known Boston musicians,
did fine work, although only one rehearsal of the Tchaikovsky works was held in the morning at the theatre. The remainder of the concert was composed of good performances
by the orchestra under Victor Herbert, and of solos by Felix
Winternitz, a brilliant young violinist. It would have been far
more satisfactory, however, if the afternoon had been devoted only to Tchaikovsky instead of introducing a bunch of
scrappy selections.

It is not often the people get a chance to have one of the
greatest of living composers in their midst, and when they
do they want to have all they can from him at the golden
moment. A Tchaikovsky overture, the concerto and suite
would have make a complete and artistic programme, which
would have given a feeling of satisfaction and perfectness
not to be attained by crowding a number of works injudi-
ciously together.

Tchaikovsky and Miss Aus der Ohe were entertained at
night by Mr. Ernst Knabe, who invited Asger Hamerick, B.
Courlaender, Harold Randolph, Miss Sophie Fernow, S.

Monroe Fabian, Richard Burmeister and a number of other Baltimore musicians to meet them. Tchaikovsky will visit the Peabody Conservatory today, and will leave Baltimore this evening. He is a fine-looking, stalwart, and dignified man, quiet and polished in his manners, and making himself understood either in broken English or one of the many European languages with which he, with the usual linguistical bent of the Russian, is thoroughly familiar. He has scant white hair and a white beard, and is younger than he looks, being fifty-one years old. His full unpronounceable name, which he whirls off in remarkable style, is Peter Ktisch [Ilyich] Tchaikovsky. His visit to America was brought about by the directors of the New York Symphony Society, who engaged him to conduct several of his own compositions at the opening of the New York Music Hall.

Baltimore American, May 16, 1891
Tchaikovsky has no superiors as a leader of musicians

At the Lyceum Theater, yesterday afternoon and evening, two ideal concerts were attended by all the lovers of music in Baltimore. The attractions were, in the afternoon, Mr. Peter Iltitisch [Ilyich] Tchaikovsky, the czar of composers and directors; Miss Adele Aus der Ohe, the unrivaled pianiste, and Felix Winternitz, the violinist, all supported by the Boston Festival Orchestra, one of the best organizations of musicians that has ever visited this city.

. . . The great interest was centered on the two great attractions, Miss Adele Aus der Ohe, and Mr. Peter Iltitisch Tchaikovsky. Miss Aus der Ohe has been heard repeatedly before in Baltimore, but never as yesterday. "Formoso!" shouted Tchaikovsky as he completed the rehearsal yesterday morning, and he would gladly have said more, when the two were recalled five times in the afternoon. Both the orchestra and the pianist delighted him.

The splendid player had but one rehearsal, and played his most difficult music at sight, and he was delighted, but his artistic nature fairly beamed with gratitude for Aus der Ohe's grand performance. She had played the work at the New York Festival, knew it by heart, and played it con amore.

Tchaikovsky was enthusiastic. From the enthusiasm shown yesterday afternoon, he knows that Baltimore is musical, and he was glad that none but musical people were present.

As for Tchaikovsky, the great Russian composer, he is also a czar among musicians and directors. His personal appearance alone shows him to be a great man. As he stands to direct, he looks as if the commander of all armies in Russia had for the moment laid aside the sword of conflict and destruction and taken up the baton of harmony and peace. He has, indeed, a "front like Mars," and "an eye to threaten or command." In fact, he does more directing with his eye alone than other directors do with all the means at their command.

In fact, it is hard for any one to be unmusical in his presence. His magnetic personality sways all who are about him. Yet he does nothing for effect. He directs, and all follow; he commands, and all instinctively obey; as though grateful in their serfdom, art governs him, and all whom he can govern. If he makes them slaves, they delight in his chains.

. . . Altogether, the two concerts by the Boston Festival Orchestra were among the best ever heard here, the ability of the musicians being shown by the fact that they played Tchaikovsky's difficult suite with but a single rehearsal, as the great composer had never seen them until this morning.

Baltimore may congratulate itself as being one of the three cities in America selected to hear Tchaikovsky, with the Boston Festival Orchestra.

Tchaikovsky and a choice company were entertained by Mr. Ernst Knabe after the concert.

DIARY   May 16, Baltimore

After awakening early and breakfasting downstairs, wrote in my diary and, not without horror, awaited Knabe, with whom I was to see the city and its sights. Mr. Suro came, a

Jew, the brother of that one who is married to the beauty,
i.e., the doctor of laws. Knabe appeared and together with
the Aus der Ohe sisters we set off knocking about Baltimore in his carriage. The weather was nasty and wet. Baltimore is a very pretty, clean city. The houses are small and
brick-red, with white marble stairs at the entrances. First we
went to the Knabe factory and surveyed his huge piano
production in every detail. All told, it was very interesting;
several machines in particular were quite appealing to me;
and the sight of lots of workers with serious, clever faces,
so clean and carefully dressed despite the rough labour,
—leaves one with a good impression. But I felt that distinctive American morning fatigue, which has oppressed me
since the first day of my arrival. With effort I could actually
speak and understand what others said to me. The glass of
beer, which Knabe offered to me after the inspection, quite
cheered me up. From there we started for the central
square with its wonderful view of the harbour and the city.
From there to the Peabody Institute. This is a huge, handsome edifice, built with the money of the rich man, Peabody. It consists of: an immense library, open to all; an art
and sculpture gallery (unusually poor and pitiable, which
doesn't prevent the Baltimorians from being proud of it),
and a conservatory. From outside, the latter is splendid. Besides a wonderful arrangement of classrooms, it has two
concert halls, its own music library, lots of instruments, etc.
Its director is Hamerick, who very courteously greeted me
and accompanied me. All the professors had been my boon
companions yesterday. Young Burmeister was burning with
a desire to play me his symphonic poem and I had to agree
to sit and listen to it in spite of my coming departure at
3 o'clock. This composition attests to the author's membership in Liszt's group of young musicians, but I wouldn't say
that it delighted me. Burmeister asked me to propagandize
it in Russia. Right after that we went home to pack and
prepare for my departure, but on the way Knabe brought
us to see some sights. This most kind giant helped me to

pack, treated Aus der Ohe and me to breakfast and champagne, and seated us in the carriage to leave for the station.
They went to Philadelphia and I to Washington, five minutes after them. Rode for only three-quarters of an hour.
Was met by Botkin. While kissing him, I had the misfortune of losing my loose front tooth, and heard with horror
that sibilants began to leave my mouth with a quite new,
distinctive whistle. Very unpleasant. Botkin drove me to the
Hotel Arlington, where he had reserved for me a superb,
fabulously comfortable suite, furnished with taste and
graceful simplicity. After refusing to go to the races, I
asked Botkin to call for me before the dinner. After his departure took a bath and changed into a dress coat. The
dinner for me was given in the Metropolitan Club, where
Botkin and his colleagues are members. The four of us
dined together: he, I, Greger, the counsellor of the Embassy, and Hansen, the first secretary. Greger is a sports-
man and just today had taken a first prize at the races.
Hansen is a musician. Both of them are very nice and likable. In manner Hansen reminds me a little of Mr. Niki-
tenko and of that Petersburg type in general. They are
young people, but Hansen is already bald. The dinner was
very gay and I enjoyed the happiness of speaking exclusively Russian, although this happiness was darkened by the
sad fact that my ch, sh, shch hiss and whistle like an old
man's. During the dinner, news arrived first by cable and
then by telephone, about the return of Ambassador Struve
from a business trip to New York, just to see me. At about
10 o'clock we started for the Embassy, where Botkin had
organized a musical evening in festive surroundings. About
one hundred people were invited. The ambassador appeared. He turned out to be an old man, very cordial, simple in manner and in general extremely congenial. The circle that gathered in the Embassy was exclusively diplomatic.
All were ambassadors with wives and daughters or func-
tionaries from the top administration. Almost all the ladies
spoke French, in consequence of which I was not especially

burdened. I talked especially long with the very clever and graceful Miss Williams. The program included my Trio and a quartet by Brahms. The piano part was performed by Secretary Hansen, who seems to be quite a good pianist. He played my Trio extremely well. The violinist was rather poor. I got acquainted with everybody. After the music an excellent cold supper was served. After most of the guests had departed, ten of us (besides Russians, there were the Belgian ambassador, and the Swedish and Austrian secretaries) sat a long while at a big round table, sipping most perfect wine. Struve apparently enjoys very much to have an extra glass of wine. He gives the impression of a man, heartbroken and sad, seeking oblivion from his sorrows in wine. At about 3 o'clock I came home, accompanied by Botkin and Hansen. Slept well.

DAY TWENTY-SECOND

DIARY   May 17, Washington

Awoke with a pleasant impression of yesterday. It was unusually soothing for me to be among Russians and have an opportunity to do without foreign languages. After drinking tea downstairs, strolled for a while in the city, which is very lovely. It is all buried in lush, spring green. After returning home (the American morning fatigue lets itself be felt nevertheless) indulged in a light nap in an unusually comfortable armchair. At about 12 o'clock Botkin called for me and we headed to Ambassador Struve's for breakfast. Since he is a widower and doesn't maintain a household, the breakfast was again in that same Metropolitan Club, where all these gentlemen spend the greater part of their lives. After breakfast I went with Botkin and Hansen in a landau to see the sights of Washington. We visited the famous obelisk (the greatest structure in the world after the Eiffel Tower); the Capitol, which provides a marvelous view of Washington, literally buried in the dense, luxuriant foliage of chestnuts, acacias, oaks, and maples; the suburban Soldier's House (a splendid park surrounding a home for veterans); and some of the best streets. Finally we returned to the Embassy. Not only the ambassador himself but all his staff live in this magnificent house. Botkin has the splendid rooms upstairs. We drank tea at his place; the most charming Struve came over and related many interesting things about his past. By the way, he is very friendly with Mitrofan Tchaikovsky, with whom he made the Khivinsky campaign. Greger also came over. I played several things with Hansen on the two pianos downstairs in the hall, and then this secretary-virtuoso beautifully played several pieces solo. We dined in the Metropolitan Club. I read in the *New York Herald* the article about me and of course saw with it the portrait by the nice reporter who visited me on my departure day.

New York Herald, May 17, 1891

Tchaikovsky on music in America. The Russian conductor vastly pleased with our audiences and musicians. How his scherzo was played. Fond of the Greek church music, and may bring a choir back with him in the fall

M. Tchaikovsky seems to be as fond of American audiences as they are of him.

"They are so warm—so sympathetic," he said to me the other day, "so like the Russian public, so quick to catch a point and so eager to show their appreciation of the good things offered them."

We were sitting in his little parlor at the Normandie, and between his nervous puffs at his cigarette the Russian conductor waxed eloquent over the great American public.

"When I say they are enthusiastic,"—he added, "I do not mean they applaud anything and everything. Far from it. They are delicately discriminating and slight the weak musical points quite as decidedly as they applaud the strong.

Their perceptions are fine and their appreciation honestly and frankly expressed." Another cigarette.

A compliment for New York

"Of course I can only speak of the New York audiences, as I know no others. But after my return from Baltimore and the South I can tell better about the public gatherings of your other cities. Not even in the music centres of Europe have I found such Musical sympathy as in New York.

"London audiences, you know, are proverbially cold, and people will tell you to seek for all that is responsive in listeners found in France, Germany and Italy. But St. Petersburg and New York are good enough for me."

Not so bad a compliment!

Our orchestras made of good stuff

"And then your musicians," he continued. "They are thoroughly capable and conscientious performers and would quite put to blush some of our players across the water in the matter of sight reading.

"Here again I can only speak of one body—your New York Symphony Society—but I sincerely trust that I may find equally good players in your other bands."

"And you were satisfied with the people to whose bands your orchestral works were intrusted at the festival?" I inquired, as still another cigarette was lighted. "Quite," came the answer between the puffs. "Quite. I must confess to a genuine surprise to find at my first rehearsal that the men had so little trouble with some of my music.

Surprised at their reading

"Now, my scherzo was by no means easy and I expected a good deal of hard work at its first trial. Judge of my astonishment then to hear it played as correctly as at the public concert.

" 'Gentlemen,' I said, 'you have rehearsed this with Mr. Damrosch.' But they all denied having seen the music before.

"As for the composition of the band, I admire the flutes and strings particularly. The flutes are beautiful and sweet and your string orchestra is sonorous and rich in quality."

"M. Tchaikovsky," I asked, suddenly changing the subject, "how much truth is there in the rumor that you are to return in the fall with a choir of Greek Church singers?" for I knew that he was an enthusiast upon this branch of music, and had shown his partiality to sacred choral writing by the selection made of his own works sung by the Oratorio Society last week.

May bring back a Russian choir

"There is a possibility that such an engagement may be made," he answered, "and the idea was first started in this way:—

"When Mr. Carnegie was in Moscow he was particularly pleased with the harmonies produced by the singers in the Cathedral, and wished his friends in New York might hear them. Now that I am coming back in the autumn, it may be that such a company may be brought back with me. I shall certainly bring the best if I bring any, and have them sing some of their own folk songs as well as their church music.

"But our church music! How beautiful it is! And did you know that until very recently no one in Russia was permitted to write anything new for the Church, and that nothing but the olden time music was allowed to be sung?"

I did not know it but I kept my ignorance to myself and allowed my host to continue.

The old and the new

"Dimitri Bortniansky, the Russian Palestrina, was the last of the old school, and long after his death, in 1825, his influence remained—a stumbling block to progress in the music of the Greek Church, and it was a long fight that finally opened the doors to the new school of music, and to Davidoff, Degteroff, Beresovsky, Tour-Tchonihoff and Wedel belongs much of the credit of the work.

"To-day these writers do nothing but compose for the Church.

"I had a little experience myself that will illustrate the high feeling about the admittance of anything new within the sacred precincts of the church.

Tchaikovsky's mass burned

"I had written a mass and given it to my publisher, who was almost immediately served with an order from court that the work must be destroyed, and, this order was speedily followed by the actual seizure of the manuscript and its destruction by fire before my publisher's very eyes.

"The music of the Greek Church of to-day, however, is beautiful beyond expression, and I trust you may have pleasure of hearing it in all of its grandeur and beauty in my home (Russia) some day," smiled my host.

His last cigarette was reduced to ashes.

"Some day," I answered, as I picked up my hat and bowed myself out.

DIARY   May 17 (continued)

At about 9 o'clock we headed for the local music school where Hansen with the student orchestra played two Beethoven concertos. In the audience were all of Hansen's friends, including my friend Miss Williams, with whom poor Hansen, as it turns out, is despondently in love. From there we went to the club again, in a very curious local two-wheeled fiacre, which belches riders out from its rear as the destination is approached. There we talked for a while and I came home accompanied by Hansen and Botkin. Had fierce nightmares before falling asleep.

DAY TWENTY-THIRD

DIARY   May 18, Washington—Philadelphia—New York

At 10:30 o'clock Botkin called for me. I paid my bill and left. Besides Botkin, Greger and Hansen also saw me off. I rode in a Pullman car. All the time I sat in the smoking compartment, being afraid of talking with the lady to whom Greger had introduced me. Arrived in Philadelphia at 3 o'clock. Visited Aus der Ohe. Had breakfast downstairs. The importunate Jew from Odessa came and got some money out of me. Went for a walk. Concert at 8 o'clock. The huge theatre was full. After the concert, was in a club according the promise I'd made before. The return to New York was very tiresome and complicated. There was stuffy air and tightness in the sleeping car. Awoke with a headache. The ride home with Aus der Ohe was endless. It has become impossible to write in detail.

Philadelphia Press, May 19, 1891
Tchaikovsky and other celebrities in a notable Musical Festival

The Academy of Music last evening contained a very large audience of music-lovers, who had congregated to do homage to one of the greatest living composers, Ilitsch [Peter Ilyich] Tchaikovsky. The term concert is too modest to express the occasion; it was a musical festival, made better than a majority of those given by Dr. Hans Richter in London, which have become almost as famous as the celebrated Bayreuth Wagnerian series. Several new and excellent virtuosi and soloists were introduced to Philadelphia audiences, and the ovations given them were well merited. . . .

The fifth number was the debut of Tchaikovsky in Philadelphia, and as soon as he was seen in the wings conducting Miss Adele Aus der Ohe upon the stage a storm of applause burst from all parts of the house, which the composer acknowledged gracefully, although with the modesty of a school boy. From that moment audience, orchestra, and soloist seemed to realize that they were in the presence of genius, and Miss Aus der Ohe rendered the composer's concerto with such artistic merit that her numerous admirers had ample cause to think that she excelled any of her previous efforts before an American audience. Her great technique and wonderful endurance stood her in good stay in this extremely difficult composition, and her masterly rendering brought forth applause from even the composer. . . .

North American, Philadelphia, May 19, 1891

The eminent Russian composer Tchaikovsky directs the performance of two of his works at the Academy of Music

There was not so large an audience as, considering of the occasion, there should have been at the Academy of Music last evening, when Peter Ilyich Tchaikovsky, the eminent Russian composer, made his first public appearance in Philadelphia, but it was at a good size considering how late it is in the season, and when the famous Russian stepped upon the stage, in company with Miss Adele Aus der Ohe, at the end of the first part of the programme, both he and the pianist received a cordial and respectful welcome.

Tchaikovsky is a distinguished-looking man, apparently about fifty years of age, and looking more like a prosperous merchant or a United States Senator than a musician. His manner is singularly unobtrusive and quite free from any kind of mannerism of affection. He seems to think of nothing but that he is there for the purpose of directing the orchestra and that duty, without any preliminary posturings or preludings, he at once proceeds to discharge. In conducting his methods are simple, clear, forcible, and masterly. He shows an entire control of his orchestral forces, and to a perfect understanding of the effects which he desired to produce, he adds the knowledge of how best they are to be obtained. He keeps the orchestra well in hand, but his discipline leaves room for the ebb and flow of emotional expression, and his reading includes a wide range of light and shade. Always free from exaggeration they are never devoid of life and color. Of course he had an advantage in this that both of the works which he conducted were of his own writing, and both were in high degree beautiful and impressive. The B-flat mi-

nor concerto is a colossal composition, enormously difficult,
full of poetry and passion; made continually striking by bi-
zarre effects, displaying a perfect mastery over the modern
orchestra and strangely moving the imagination with its melodic beauty and rich, resounding harmonies. It is great music of the most modern school and spirit, and it was greatly
played by Miss Aus der Ohe, whose mere memorization of
such a long and difficult work, was a wonderful feat. She
played it with splendid breadth and power and spirit, and
received the congratulations of all present, including the
composer. The other of Tchaikovsky's works rendered was
a suite for string orchestra, which also made a deeply favorable impression. It is on a smaller scale than the concerto,
but is no less strikingly original in idea and shows an alike
inexhaustible flow of melody and invention. Both it and the
concerto were effectively played by the orchestra, which,
though small, was of good quality. The soloists at the concert
besides Miss Aus der Ohe were Miss Rose Stewart, a pleasing
soprano; Mr. Myron Whitney, Mr. Felix Winternitz, a clever
young violinist, and Mr. Victor Herbert, the cello virtuoso.
They all deserve a word of praise.

Daily Evening Telegraph, Philadelphia, May 19, 1891
Tchaikovsky's concert

Mr. Tchaikovsky, the famous Russian composer, was the recipient of a Philadelphia ovation last night which was alike
an honor to the community and the artist. We have said it
would have been a local reproach if this truly distinguished
man should fail of recognition in a community of the size
and culture of Philadelphia, but so uncertain is popular favor and attention that nothing could be predicated of the
result of last night's concert with certainty. As events turned
out, however, all fears were seen to be groundless. The
Academy was filled with a company of a quite exceptional
kind, and the reception of Mr. Tchaikovsky had all the
warmth that could have been hoped for. The impression from

a popular view, made by the composer was instantly favorable, though Tchaikovsky has not the professional air which most people possibly expected. He looks like a broker and clubman rather than an artist. He seems to be rising sixty, but is well preserved and active. He is of middle height, slim, erect, with silvery gray hair and beard, florid complection, and small but piercing and expressive blue eyes;—a self-contained and dignified personage, not without grace, but clearly giving no attention to stage niceties—altogether an attractive personality, if somewhat disconcerting to those who expected a more pronounced slavic type, such as Rubinstein. It was agreeable to see the way in which he assumed that the great audience had not assembled to do him personal honor, but to hear certain pieces of music in which he was merely concerned with the interpretation. He conveyed this idea without affection, nor too much of brusqueness. Taking up the baton without delay, he ceased at once to be the guest, and was but one of a company of artists engaged in performing to a Philadelphia audience. His work at the desk (consisting of the leading of his Pianoforte concerto in B-flat minor, and his Suite for string orchestra) showed good, if not remarkable, powers as a conductor.

He had a firm grasp of the subject at all times, and one felt the confidence of the players, that there was no instant of wavering or uncertainty. In leading, Mr. Tchaikovsky looks minutely, perhaps too much so, after all the details of entrance and expression, but there are no special points to be noted in his manner, unless it be the peculiarity of beating from the wrist rather than with the full arm—not an invariable custom, of couse, but frequent with him and perhaps a concomitant of his piano habit. Both works were given with a delightful precision which yet did not interfere with their strange and original rhythms. The Concerto was especially successful, and it is indeed a splendid composition, fresh and ideal, and with new ideas blossoming out to the very close. The Suite, owing to its position on the programme—coming

at the end of a long, warm evening, when people were growing tired—and with insufficient strength of strings, was not
heard to quite the same advantage. The fifteen or sixteen
instruments employed, while they might be sufficient in a
smaller hall, had not proper body for such an auditorium as
the Academy. In the concerto, Miss Aus der Ohe won a
marked triumph, carrying a part of great difficulty with consummate power and finish. The lady has never appeared, we
think, with such splendid artistic effect in this vicinity as on
this occasion. . . .

DAY TWENTY-FOURTH

DIARY   May 19, New York

   Slept till 9 o'clock and my head got better. Visits from
Reinhard and Holls. Grew dull from fatigue and bustle;
didn't understand a thing and only kept my energy up
by thinking of the coming departure tomorrow. Letters
with requests for autographs exhaust me. At 12:30
o'clock headed for Mayer's. Wrote that notorious letter-
advertisement without the phrase about superiority. Had
breakfast with Reinhard and him in an Italian restaurant.
At home awaited the composer, Bruno Klein. He appeared
and played me several of his lovely pieces. At 4 o'clock Mr.
Holls came for me. With him and the Aus der Ohe sisters,
headed for Central Station, joined the Reno couple, and
rode along the Hudson. In half an hour we got out of the
train and, getting in charabanc, started for Holls's dacha
along a marvelous, scenic road. This summer house-villa, of
quite elegant construction, stands on the high bank of the
Hudson. The view opening from the balcony, the pavilion,
and especially from the roof of the house, is incomparable.
At 6 o'clock we sat down to dine. The conversation was
lively and I did not feel oppressed for indeed what could I

endure at this time with my departure so close!!! Aus der Ohe played after dinner. At 10:30 o'clock we got in the charabanc one more time and returned home by train. Reno talked about my engagement for the next year. I called on Aus der Ohe and bid farewell to them. Packed.

DAY TWENTY-FIFTH

New York World, May 20, 1891
The world of music

. . . The Composer's Club has arranged to have a Russian night of music at the Concert Hall of the Metropolitan Opera House this evening, when M. Tchaikovsky, the Russian composer, will be given a reception. It is rather strange that a composer of M. Tchaikovsky's reputation and genius should have been so long in the city without having any special honors rendered to him by the representative lights of literature, music and art. The honor to be paid him by the Composer's Club is the result of a proper spirit of appreciation of the Russian's greatness. M. Tchaikovsky sails on Saturday for Europe and will in all probability return next season.

Musical Courier, May 20, 1891
The raconteur

So it is. Tchaikovsky is with us, a noble thinker in tone, who will be honored when these United States have had another centennial celebration, but Benny Harrison, third-rate President and fourth-rate Indiana lawyer gets columns in every paper in the country simply because he is making a junketing tour!

It makes me sick. And forsooth if I express my keen admiration for beautiful music I am paid for it! Yes, I am paid for it and a thousand times repaid for it, for can I not listen to Tchaikovsky's music, and is that not magnificent pay for my petty praise?

Let us salute Peter Ilyich Tchaikovsky. He does not compose like Bach, Beethoven, nor yet Wagner, but he has given us new thoughts, a broader vision, a new gleam of beauty from that wonderful ocean called music; so Salutumus te, Petrum Tchaikovskiensem, and a short shrift for your detractors.

DIARY   May 20

The little old librettist. It was most regrettable to tell him of my reluctance to write an opera on his text. He was clearly upset. As soon as he left, Dannreuther appeared for me in order to drive me to the rehearsal of the Quartet and Trio, which are to be performed at the gala concert in the Composer's Club tonight. We had to ride quite far. The Quartet was played rather poorly and the Trio even worse, for the pianist (Mr. Huss, modest and cowardly) is quite inferior and can't even count. At home had no time to do anything toward preparing for departure. In a carriage started for lunch at Reno's place. More than ever, they, that is, Mrs. Reno and the three daughters, treated me enthusiastically and cordially. The eldest (Anna, married) presented me with a luxurious cigarette case. Mrs. Reno—with lots of perfume; Alice and her sister—with cookies for my trip. Afterwards hurried to Hyde's. Mrs. Hyde was waiting for me. Again much genuine enthusiasm, expressed with her characteristic humor. At last could begin packing for home—detestable occupation. Besides, my back pained me cruelly. Tired, I went to Mayer's. I treated Reinhard and him to an excellent dinner at Martelli's. At 8 o'clock hastened home to change clothes. At 8:30 Mason came for me. The Composer's Club is not a club of composers, as I initially thought, but a special musical society, the goal of which is to provide concerts of works by one composer from time to time.

New York Daily Tribune, May 21, 1891

The reception for Tchaikovsky—A pleasant farewell to the popular composer

The Composer's Club gave an enjoyable and successful reception to P. Tchaikovsky, the Russian composer, at the assembly rooms of the Metropolitan Opera House last night. Mr. Tchaikovsky has enjoyed many pleasant evenings, since he has been here, but he will probably remember last night as one of the pleasantest of all. Many people well known in musical circles in this city united in honoring the popular composer, and in wishing him a safe voyage home and a speedy return to this country. He will sail for Europe to-day on the Fuerst Bismarck, of the Hamburg-American Line.

A number of people were introduced to Mr. Tchaikovsky in the anterooms before the entertainment began, and when he took his seat in the assembly-room he was warmly applauded. There was a brilliant gathering of people, and the hall presented an attractive appearance.

The entertainment consisted of performances of Mr. Tchaikovsky's music of the Beethoven String Quartet. Gerrit Smith was the director of the evening. . . . Each programme had an excellent likeness on it of the guest of the evening, which was taken for the occasion and which made an appropriate souvenir of the occasion. . . . Mr. Smith read an interesting sketch of Mr. Tchaikovsky's life, in which he spoke of the pre-eminence that this composer had given to Russian music in the musical world and also paid a high tribute to Mr. Tchaikovsky himself. He is a man of striking appearance of medium size, of florid complexion with white hair, mustache and beard. There is no dreamy expression in his eyes; on the contrary, he has a wide-awake, keen look, and his movements are animated and graceful. He responded in a few happy words which were warmly received.

DIARY   May 20 (continued)

The evening was dedicated to me and took place in the splendid hall of the Metropolitan Opera. I sat in the first row. They played the E-flat Minor Quartet, the Trio, sang romances, some of which were beautifully performed (Mrs. Alwes), etc. The program was too long. In the middle of the evening, Mr. Smith read me an address. I responded briefly in French; ovation of course. One lady threw a gorgeous bouquet of roses right into my face. Became acquainted with great number of people, including our General Consul. After the end I had to talk with a hundred people and write a hundred autographs. At last, fully exhausted and suffering severely from my backache, I started for home. Since the ship is leaving at 5 o'clock, I have to board it in the evening. Packed hastily, changed; Reno, Mayer, and Reinhard were present in time for it. Downstairs we drank two bottles of champagne; after that, saying good-bye to the hotel's personnel, rode to the ship. We rode for a long while. The ship was as magnificent as *La Bretagne*. I have an officer's cabin, i.e., officers of these ships have the right to sell their accommodations—but they fleece one cruelly. I paid $300 (1500 francs) for my cabin!!! But then it is indeed good and commodious. Said farewell to my dear American friends and soon after that went to sleep. Slept badly and heard the ship starting out at 5 o'clock. Came out of my cabin when we passed the Statue of Liberty.

New York Herald, May 24, 1891
Tchaikovsky in America

If we were count up all the men and women of genius now adorning the world how long would the list be?

Should we be able to name twelve or ten or six such people? Men whose claim to the high honor would not be disputed by even the most skeptical and cold?

Let us try.

To head the list we should, of course, have Bismarck. Then might come Edison and Tolstoi, Sarah Bernhardt and perhaps Ibsen, with Herbert Spencer and two great composers—Dvorak and Tchaikovsky. The right of Tchaikovsky to a place on the roll will hardly, we think, be denied. He has that noblest of gifts—the gift creative. His works have unquestionable strength, originality and poetry.

This genius has been within our gates—has been here, indeed, for three weeks or more. And how have we shown our recognition of his presence? How have we honored this great Russian composer?

We have made much of such bright but far less wondrous lights, of actresses and artists of mere talent. But, apart from one reception and a few rounds of applause, we fail to see that public tribute or that private honor New York paid to Tchaikovsky.

Tchaikovsky is a modest, unassuming man. But no genius is unconscious of his genius.

What impression of New York will he take back to Europe, where his name is both a glory and a power?

III

To America Again?

May 21, Atlantic Ocean

Ignoring my desperate backache, forced myself to dress,
drank tea downstairs, and walked about the ship in order
to familiarize myself with the location of its parts. There is
a great host of passengers,—but this society has another
character from the one that sailed on *La Bretagne*. The most
striking difference is that there are no emigrants here. At
eight o'clock we were called for breakfast. My place had already been pointed out to me before. My neighbor is a
middle-aged gentleman, who immediately started up a conversation. All morning I slept. Am indifferent to the view
of the ocean. Am thinking of the coming journey with a
feeling, not of horror, but of boredom: I would like it to
end sooner! The steamer is flying with a special rapidity; it
is the new, luxurious *Fürst Bismarck,* making its first return
voyage. Last week it sailed from Hamburg to New York,
making the passage in only 6 days and 14 hours. God grant
that we travel the great distance just as fast. When in motion it is not as smooth as the *Bretagne*. So far the weather is
wonderful. At lunch became closer acquainted with my "vis-
à-vis." This gentleman is of indeterminate nationality (probably a Jew—as luck would have it, I told him the story of
the annoying Jew), who speaks all languages perfectly. He
lives in Dresden and trades tobacco "en gros." Either he has
already managed to find out who I am, or, if he speaks the

truth, he indeed saw me conduct in New York. Anyway he showered me with compliments and is rapturous in the presence of my celebrity and talent. Accustomed in New York to speaking constantly, even when disposed to be silent, I began to bear the man's company without difficulty, which in the morning had so oppressed me. The singer Antonia Mielke, who I knew to be on this vessel and of whom I was a little afraid, fortunately does not sit at the same table with me, although she apparently tried to arrange it so. I saw her just before dinner. After lunch I wanted to read, but instead of that fell asleep and slept three full hours. On the whole I slept surprisingly much today. In the evening, soon after dinner, a drowsiness again fell upon me so that I retired at about ten o'clock and slept till 7 o'clock in the morning. Nothing particular happened during the course of the day. A Mr. Aronson came up to me with his young wife to make my acquaintance. He is the owner of the Casino Theater, which is a favourite of von Bülow's, as is clear from the autograph album he sent me several days ago for me to write in my name and a line of music. The steward of my cabin, Schreider, is a most kind young German. The table is served by two equally congenial Germans—this is very important to me. On the whole, I am pleased with the steamer, my cabin, and the food. Since there are no emigrants, I can walk on the lower deck, which is quite pleasant, for I don't meet my first-class companions there and can have silence.

May 22

The day was not marked by anything special. The weather was a little foggy, as usual near the "Banks" of Newfoundland, but calm. I have already accustomed myself to the ship and public and my relations are now settled. I keep myself to the side and, thanks to my wonderful cabin, where it's possible to walk without difficulty, I feel much freer than on the *Bretagne*. Can talk to my neighbor at the table without strain. With my other neighbors, an American family,—I have, so to speak, a nodding acquaintance. Once a day I talk with Mielke about the opera, singers, and Petersburg, where she sang two years ago at the Livadia. To Aronson and his wife I only nod. Of the other three hundred passengers I so far associate with none. I go to the smoking room and watch as they play cards. My neighbor at table plays skat there all day. Mornings I come into the salon, when nobody is there. An elegant Steinway piano stands there. They have a rather good music library. My works are also there. The course of the day is as follows: in the morning, after dressing, I ring for Schreider, who brings me a cup of tea. At 8 o'clock: first breakfast. I eat an omelet and drink tea with pfannkuchen. The tea is good. Then I walk on the lower deck, work, and read. By work I mean the sketches for my future symphony.[38] At 12 o'clock the "tam-tam" sounds:—it's the call to second breakfast. The two hot dishes and a great number of cold ones are served. After that I walk again, read, and talk with Mielke. At 6 o'clock, dinner. It lasts till 7:30. Then I drink coffee in the "Rauchzimmer" and wander about the ship, especially on the lower deck, where there are only third-classers, and not many of them. Retire early. Two times a day an orchestra plays. It consists of stewards of the second class (of whom there are about 16) and performs quite well, although the repertory is poor. They play first at 2 o'clock, and then at dinner. I marvel at the sea, only a little. It is magnificent but I am filled too much with yearning for home. I feel perfect. My appetite is greater than it's been for a long time. At all three meals I devour an enormous amount of food. This night for some reason slept badly; constantly waking up. Am now reading Tatishchev's book, *Alexandre et Napoleon*.

May 23

I was so often told in New York that the sea is admirable at this time of year, that I came to believe it. Oh, what a disappointment! Since morning the weather's been getting bad; the rain came, a wind started blowing, and in the evening, a storm. A terrible night! Didn't sleep. Sat on the sofa. Toward morning dozed off.

May 24

A disgusting day! The weather is atrocious. The sea is raging. Seasickness. Vomited. All day I ate but one orange.

May 25

Yesterday evening, completely exhausted from fatigue and indisposition, I fell asleep on my little sofa still dressed and slept through the night in this way. Today there is less tossing, and yet the weather is abominable. My nerves are inexpressibly strained and irritated by noise and cracks, which do not cease for even a moment. Will I truly venture to suffer through it all once more?

As the day went on, the tossing subsided and bit by bit the weather became very good. An aversion for the company of passengers came over me; the very appearance of them now angers and terrifies me. I remain in my cabin, almost without going out. However, during the meals, besides my usual conversationalist, the tobacconist, I now speak in English with the American group sitting at our table. They are quite nice people, particularly the tall, plump lady. They are going to northern Norway to view the midnight sun. From there they are off to Petersburg.

May 26

The night was splendid, quiet, moonlit. Having read for a long while in my cabin, I roamed about on deck. It was amazingly pleasant. All, without exception, were sleeping, and I was the sole one of 300 passengers in first class to come out and marvel at the night. The beauty is indescribable; no words could convey it. It is strange now to recall that horrifying Sunday night, when everything in my cabin,

Walter Damrosch, 1891   Andrew Carnegie, 1891

Mrs. Andrew Carnegie, silver trowel in hand, presides over the laying of the Carnegie Hall cornerstone on May 11, 1890. Andrew Carnegie (whose face is partly obscured by the ropes holding the cornerstone) can be seen standing to the left of the man in the center wearing the apron and top hat. Mrs. Carnegie, a devoted amateur musician, strongly favored the building of the new concert hall and helped persuade her husband to fund it. (*Courtesy of the Carnegie Hall Co.*)

Carnegie Hall as it looked on opening night, May 5, 1891
(*Courtesy of the Carnegie Hall Co.*)

The entrance to Carnegie Hall
(*Courtesy of the Carnegie Hall Co.*)

Fifth Avenue, New York City, ca. 1900

Tchaikovsky in the garden of his house in the village Frolovskoe

Peter Jurgenson

Nadezhda Filaretovna von Meck

The Tchaikovsky brothers (left to right): Anatoly, Nikolay, Ippolit, Peter, Modest

Tchaikovsky and his nephew
Vladimir (Bob) Davidov

TSCHAIKOWSKY IS HERE.

THE RUSSIAN COMPOSER ARRIVED ON LA BRETAGNE YESTERDAY.

The great Russian composer, Peter Tschaikowsky, arrived on the French steamer La Bretagne yesterday and immediately upon seeing to a few small pieces of luggage was driven to his hotel.

The traveller carries his years well and, but for the white in his beard and hair, looks every whit ten years younger than his biographers rate him.

He comes to take an active part in the May Festival, to be held in the New Carnegie Hall during the first week in May, when he will conduct a number of his own compositions.

As a composer Tschaikowsky holds a position in Russia equal, if not superior, to that of Rubinstein himself, although the latter has a wider European reputation as a pianist.

"I was seventeen years of age," said the composer, "when I made the acquaintance of my sing

PETER TSCHAIKOWSKY, THE RUSSIAN COMPOSER.

ing master, Piccioli, and his influence over me was enormous. Up to this day I hear the melodies of Bellini with tears in my eyes."

As with many others who rank high in his profession, Tschaikowsky began his young manhood as a lawyer's clerk, and not until he had passed his majority was he allowed to enter the conservatorium founded by Rubinstein.

In 1865 he was appointed Professor of Composition in the Moscow Conservatoire and served there until his illness in 1877, which compelled him to resign. Since then he has lived exclusively devoted to composition.

"Tschaikovsky Is Here," from the
New York *Herald*, April 27, 1891

Peter Tchaikovsky, 1891

Adele Aus der Ohe, 1891

Face page of the program from the five-day festival that marked the official opening of Carnegie Hall in 1891 (*Courtesy of the Carnegie Hall Co.*)

MUSIC FESTIVAL

In Celebration of the Opening of

MUSIC HALL

CORNER 57TH STREET & 7TH AVENUE,

MAY 5, 6, 7, 8, and 9, 1891.

The Symphony Society Orchestra,

The Oratorio Society Chorus,

BOYS' CHOIR OF 100, (Wenzel Raboch, Choirmaster.)

AND THE FOLLOWING ARTISTS:

P. TSCHAIKOWSKY, the eminent Russian composer, who will conduct several of his own works.

FRAU ANTONIA MIELKE, Soprano.
MLLE. CLEMENTINE DE VERE, Soprano.
MRS. GERRIT SMITH, Soprano.
MRS. TH. J. TOEDT, Soprano.
MISS ANNA LUELLA KELLY, Soprano.
MRS. KOERT KRONOLD, Soprano.
FRAU MARIE RITTER-GOETZE, Contralto.
MRS. CARL ALVES, Contralto.
MRS. CLAPPER-MORRIS, Contralto.

SIGNOR ITALO CAMPININI, Tenor.
HERR ANDREAS DIPPEL, Tenor.
MR. THOMAS EBERT, Tenor.
HERR THEODOR REICHMANN, Baritone.
HERR EMIL FISCHER, Bass.
HERR CONRAD BEHRENS, Bass.
MR. ERICSON BUSHNELL, Bass.
FRL. ADELE AUS DER OHE, Pianist.
MR. FRANK L. SEALY, Organist.

WALTER DAMROSCH, - CONDUCTOR.

THE MUSIC HALL COMPANY OF NEW YORK, Limited.

MORRIS RENO, President.

FREDERICK WILLIAM HOLLS, Secretary.   STEPHEN M. KNEVALS, Treasurer.

DIRECTORS.

John W. Aitkin,	Frederick Wm. Holls,	Sherman W. Knevals,
Andrew Carnegie,	Wm. S. Hawk,	Morris Reno,
Walter J. Damrosch,	Stephen M. Knevals,	William B. Tuthill.

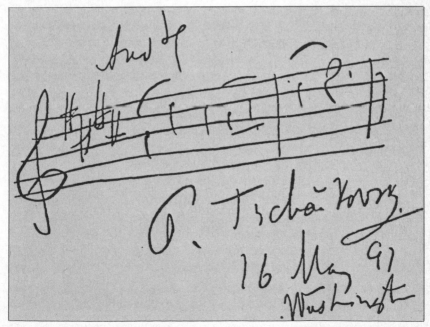

Front and back of the program card for the concert at the Russian Embassy in Washington, D.C., with a quotation from the second movement of the Trio, op. 50 (*Courtesy of the Library of Congress*)

even the trunk, rolled from one corner to the other; when some terrifying jolts, that had caused a shudder and seemed to be the ship's last efforts to battle the fury, filled my heart with an agonizing fright; when, to cap this horror, the electric lamp crashed into smithereens! I promised myself that night not to sail any more on the sea. But my steward, Schreider, says that always during bad weather he promises himself to quit ship service and always after returning to harbor he longs for the sea and feels bored without it. Probably the same will happen to me. Finally the weather became splendid today. The passengers are talking about a concert today in the salon and pestering me to play. That is what poisons a sea voyage: the obligatory acquaintance with the company of passengers.

May 27

The weather has become beautiful. From time to time we have had sprinkles of rain. The more we neared La Manche, the more the sea became agitated. Full hundreds of small fishing vessels came in sight of the ship. About 2 p.m. the English coast appeared; in some places it is rocky and picturesque, elsewhere it is flat and blanketed with fresh spring grass. Besides these things, nothing special has happened, except for an after-dinner ball, at which I was present not more than five minutes. My circle of acquaintances has greatly increased. Fortunately I can hide in my excellent cabin for hours. At 2 a.m. we arrived in Southampton. Here a few of the passengers, among them the Aronsons and the American family going to Norway, left. I woke and came out to watch the departure of the little vessel. Marveled at the splendid sunrise.

May 28

After Southampton and the Isle of Wight, slept again and woke at 7 o'clock, slightly cold. The weather continues to be perfect. For most of the morning was on deck in the company of my new friends, the Tiedemann brothers, admiring the coast of England and the view of the many ships and sailing vessels, scurrying through the channel. Folkestone and Dover appeared for a moment. The German sea is very animated. At night Helgoland in the distance.

May 29

Early in the morning we came to Cuxhaven. At 6 o'clock, we were given breakfast. At 8 we changed for a small ship and with sounds of a march and shouts of "Hurrah!" we approached customs. A very long inspection and wait for the train. I sat in a coupe with Hulse, the Tiedemann brothers, and Aramburo, the singer. At 12 o'clock we arrived in Hamburg. I put in at the Hotel St. Petersburg.

From Hamburg Tchaikovsky left for Berlin on May 18/30 and then to Petersburg, where he arrived on May 20, 1891 (old style). There he spent a week among those closest to him and was, according to his brother Modest, "very joyful and radiant." However he was anxious to return to the daily pursuit that made him happiest, that is, composing, and on May 29 he at last returned to his home, preceded by his belongings, which Alexey Sofronov had moved in advance. Tchaikovsky's new home was in the village of Maidanovo near Klin, a place he had occupied several years before, until 1887. On that very day Tchaikovsky began to write letters.

PETER TCHAIKOVSKY TO IPPOLIT TCHAIKOVSKY

Maidanovo, May 29, 1891

Dear friend Ippolit,

I believe it will be of interest to you and Sonia to know where and how I am, and therefore am hastening to inform you that today I came back home. I sailed from New York on May 21 and was on the ocean only seven and a half days. The voyage was, like the first one, quite safe although both times we received a good tossing. From Hamburg (I went by a German ship) I proceeded directly to Petersburg, where I spent eight extremely pleasant days. Although they gave me a splendid reception in New York and although I saw much in America that was of great interest, I fervently desired to be home and cannot express how happy I was when I found myself in Russia. Now I shall set to work. According to my promise I must compose an opera and ballet for the 1892–93 season and besides write several compositions, planned long ago.

What plans do you have? Where shall you spend the summer, autumn, and winter? How are you? In August I want to be at Kolia's, in Ukolovo. Will you come there? Write or ask Sonia to answer these questions for me. Modest, Bob, and Sania Litke will come to me on June 2 and stay for two days. I know nothing about Anatoly; he answered neither letters nor telegrams. Perhaps he is on his way to Revel. I am living in the old hearth in the village of Maidanovo. I am perfectly well. I embrace you hard, kiss Sonia's hand; and give Tasia a warm embrace.

Yours,
P. Tchaikovsky

PETER TCHAIKOVSKY TO NIKOLAY TCHAIKOVSKY

Maidanovo, May 29, 1891

My dear friend Nikolasha,

I think you and Olia will not find it uninteresting to learn where and how I am. I left New York on May 21, precisely on your nameday and birthday, and sailed quite safely for seven and a half days to Hamburg. Only two days and especially one night were bad; for all the remaining time the weather was splendid. In Hamburg I spent a night and then hurried via Berlin to Petersburg. I fervently desired to find myself among close ones a bit sooner. In Peter[sburg] stayed for eight days, which went by quite pleasantly. I regret only that you were not there. On the whole I am satisfied with the American trip, that is, I enjoy recalling my success and the cordial welcome, given to me everywhere. They earnestly request that I come again. It may indeed happen that in a year I'll again be in America, where for once I'll be able to make a lot of money. Now I bring back very little at all, for I've wasted too much. Today came here, to Maidanovo, to the very house where I had lived before. Beginning tomorrow, I'll settle down to hard work. Late in the summer, without fail, shall be in Ukolovo. In a day or two, Modest, Bob, and Sania Litke will be here for a short time. I have seen neither hide nor hair of Anatoly. I embrace you hard, kiss Olia's hands and hug my dear George close to my heart. Be healthy!

Yours,
P. Tchaikovsky

PETER TCHAIKOVSKY TO VLADIMIR NAPRAVNIK

Maidanovo, May 29, 1891

Golubchik Volodia,

I've completely forgotten whether I answered your dear letter from New York or only intended. If I have not, for God's sake, forgive me! During the last days of my stay there I was in such a mad bustle that it was difficult to find time for letters and I didn't keep to my correspondence regularly. So, if am guilty, forgive me. I will now impart brief news about myself. I sailed from New York on May 21, St. Nikolin's Day. The trip took less than eight days. In Hamburg and Berlin I rested. In Petersburg spent a few very pleasant days. Despite my American success and the great number of strong impressions I experienced, all the time I was racked with homesickness and with all my soul craved to come back home. This morning I came home. Tomorrow I shall go to work. I don't remember whether or not I wrote your Papa that I'd declined to compose the ballet and opera for the next season in view of the impossibility of composing well in such a short time. But with all the more pleasure I'll instead take up this work for the season of 1892–93. I am awfully fond of the opera's plot and, if am not mistaken, I can well fulfill the accepted task, provided that I do not hurry too much. All summer I will stay in the country. The day after tomorrow, Modest, Bob, and Sania Litke will be coming to stay with me for several days. Will your Papa go to Prague? I would like it terribly much if he did so. I am certain that a tremendous triumph awaits him, and I think that he will carry away a good impression of Prague for his whole life. I didn't visit your Mama in Peter[sburg] for I was told that she went somewhere for five days. What are you doing? Write a note and tell me how you all are. Embrace your father hard for me; kiss Mama's hands, bow to your sisters and give to Kotia my friendly kiss. I embrace you, my dear!

Don't be cross.

Yours,
P. Tchaikovsky

Have I addressed this properly?

PETER TCHAIKOVSKY TO WILLIAM VON SACHS

Maidanovo, Klin, near Moscow, May 29, 1891

My dear friend,

I've just come home and found your nice letter. Thank you very much! I also thank you for your portrait; although little it is quite true to life. I made a perfect nonstop trip from Hamburg to Petersburg. Of course, my stay in New York left me unforgettable memories and with great pleasure I ponder over a second excursion to your terrain,—but this doesn't prevent me from returning with pleasure to my homeland and meeting my relatives. Upon reflection I've decided to stay at home in tranquility for the whole summer and therefore not go to Bayreuth, despite my intense desire to hear *Parsifal* and see you. I have to work; for too long a time I've done nothing. In order to fulfill all that's been promised, I must remain at home for a few months without interruption. It's too bad that you cannot be present at the first performance of *The Queen of Spades* in Hamburg. I would be so glad to meet you there! Why is it so necessary that you return to New York by September 1? I dare to think that my opera may interest you. I hope you will hear it in New York or in Germany upon your return. There's been talk about an invitation to me but it is not decided yet. Anyway I am telling you "Goodbye." Inform me from time to time about yourself!

I embrace you.

> Your devoted friend,
> P. Tchaikovsky

If I suddenly change my resolution and decide to go to Bayreuth, I will let you know immediately.

PETER TCHAIKOVSKY TO ANNA MERKLING

> Maidanovo, June 3, 1891

Golubushka Ania,

Please send my American diary here, after reading it, by book rate. In order to save yourself time, call on O. I. Yurgenson and ask him to send it. I need it for Anatoly, who will be here shortly. I kiss your hands.

PETER TCHAIKOVSKY TO PETER JURGENSON

> Maidanovo, June 3, 1891

Dear friend,

At last I am home and awfully glad to be finished with my wanderings. In general I am very satisfied with my trip to America, i.e., I enjoy remembering how enthusiastically they received me, how obliging, affectionate, friendly every-

one (except your Tretbar) was to me. But all the time I was
staying there, I yearned and craved for home in the depth
of my heart. I left having promised to come to America
again and even gave them the hope of my coming in January of next winter. But I will in no way elect to do that; this
winter I want to stay at home and work, and thus would
rather go for the next season, that is, 1892–93. Of course,
on this occasion I would go only on condition of a very
profitable fee, so as to lay aside several thousand roubles.
This time I brought home only 1000 roubles, which I have
already managed to waste at an incredible rate. One of
these days I'll have to turn to Pavel Ivanovich Jurasov.
Your Tretbar dealt with me very oddly. At a time when
many people quite alien to me welcomed me and took care
of me from the first till last minute in every possible way,
Mr. Tretbar chose to wait for my visit. And when at last I
considered myself obliged to visit him and, upon finding
him out, left my card—he did not honor me with a return
visit. But to hell with him. I had no need of him at all and
I don't regret a bit that I did not make his acquaintance.

Aside from New York I have been in Niagara, spent two
very pleasant days in Washington with the Russian embassy
personnel, and also was in Philadelphia and Baltimore,
where I conducted the touring Boston orchestra. My trip
back was made in the new and magnificent Hamburg ship
Fürst Bismarck. My voyage was successful but two days of it
were rough. Then I went straight to Petersburg and, as it
turned out, somewhere on the way met you. In Petersburg
I spent a week. Now I am at work in Maidanovo. You are
probably aware that I refused to prepare the opera and the
ballet for the coming season. They are postponed till the
next season. Now I am writing the second act of the ballet,
upon completion of which I will begin the opera *King
René's Daughter*. During the winter and spring I will in good
time orchestrate both scores (the opera is in one act), complete the piano scores, do the proofreading and by spring
we can both present all this to the Directorate. Besides *Voe-*

voda, which I will orchestrate in the summer as well. As to
the orchestration of this piece, I have a favor to ask of you.
I discovered a new orchestral instrument in Paris, something like a cross between a little piano and a glockenspiel
with a divinely marvelous sound. I want to use this instrument in the symphonic poem *Voevoda* and in the ballet. For
the ballet it will not be needed before autumn of 1892, but
for *Voevoda* it will be indispensable to the coming season,
for I've promised to conduct this piece in Petersburg at the
Musical Society and probably will also manage to perform it
in Moscow. It is called "Celeste Mustel" and costs 1200
francs. It can be bought in Paris from the inventor, Mr.
Mustel. I want to ask you to order this instrument. You lose
nothing by it for you can rent it out for all concerts where
Voevoda will be played. And afterwards you can sell it to the
Directorate of theaters when they'll be needing it for the
ballet. I myself am ready to order the "Celeste" except that,
first of all, I don't know the procedure for ordering and
second, where will I keep it and how would I hire it out
and later sell it to the Directorate? I am not at all clear
about this. So, if you agree to comply with my request,
write P. I. Jurasov that he should contact Mr. Mustel and
order the Celeste. In my turn when I come to Moscow, I
will give Mustel's address and all necessary instructions to
Jurasov or Nina Valerianovna. And since the instrument
will be needed in Petersburg earlier than in Moscow, I
would like it to be sent from Paris to Osip Ivanovich. But at
the same time I am anxious that it not be shown to anyone,
for I am afraid that Rimsky-Korsakov and Glazunov will
sniff it out and make use of its extraordinary effects before
me. In several days I will be in Moscow and can warn them
at your office of all these things. Please be so kind as to
give them orders to deal with Mr. Mustel. I predict that this
new instrument will have a colossal effect.

I address this letter to you in Kissingen poste restante
but am somewhat afraid that it will not reach you.

How are you? For a long time I have had no news from you. Maidanovo is a sorry sight. Aside from the consequences of a fire, everything else is headed for destruction, and even my house is badly askew.

I have not seen any of the Moscow people. Ziloty left the conservatory, which was to be expected.

I embrace you.

P. Tchaikovsky

PETER JURGENSON TO PETER TCHAIKOVSKY

Kissingen, June 8, 1891

Dear friend,

Welcome home! As to your success in America I did read and hear of it but these German rascals are stifling news of it on account of their Russophobia. All newspapers are filled with curses against Russia and Russians. Were we not such milksops, no Russians would be seen in Germany, just as no Frenchmen are seen here. I struggled in both Berlin and Leipzig and declared in Dresden that I would never come back to the hotel if they didn't subscribe to Russian newspapers, etc. You are of course smiling at my jingoism but, I think, if 5 percent of all traveling Russians were the same kind of pioneer, we would be more respected in Germany. You can't imagine to what lengths Germans have gone eliminating foreign words! Every day I laugh at and mock the "menu"—everything is translated and sometimes is quite ridiculous.

Thank God! The opening is finished. And you've brought a thousand roubles—that's money too. Of course, if you go to America again, don't go for less than half a million!

My Tretbar was simply not in New York,—I can't explain his silence otherwise. He had asked that I send him a telegram and said he would come from his *Landsitz* [Ger., country seat]. Perhaps he could not get away—his summer house lies a distance of a few hundred miles from New York. We'll see. He could not act so rudely on purpose.

I am awfully glad that we'll have the possibility to engrave, correct, and print *Voevoda, Hamlet,* and the opera calmly, without pressure. Of course, I will order the Celeste Mustel with pleasure. Just give Mustel's address to Jurasov. Let's keep it a secret—this is entirely necessary in order that others do not make use of this effect before us. As to my address, I always arrange things so that letters reach me.

As to the score of *Onegin,* it would be good of you to scan the Khristoforov's copy—is everything in order? I want to print and fervently desire that you be satisfied with the new edition. It seems to me Khristoforov has done nothing. I am printing the score of *The Queen of Spades* including Ratter's share too—therefore, with the German text. Ratter's business won't be much to count on in the future, so I ask you: do you have anything against Bock? He is a powerful person, precisely in the business of opera, and can deal apart from Palliny with his heavy and everlasting ties.

I am sorry about the Conservatory and the Musical Society in Moscow. Complete discord. Nikolay Grigorievich may turn over in his grave on account of our affairs. Everything is coming apart, and God knows whether the new uniform will fit better. I don't trust the rigidity of personal tyranny, especially if it is not of Rubinstein's kind. Ziloty and Busony left, and Vasily Ilyich will certainly replace them by not independent persons. Well, let it pass.

There is bad weather here all the time. From here I will go to travel a bit and then will go to Holland, probably Scheveningen to sit by the sea.

Good-bye, be well.

Yours,
P. Jurgenson

P.S. Yesterday Natalia Nikolaevna arrived and now I will not feel so lonely. Sends her regards.

Neither the joy of homecoming nor the happiness of work could smother the burning pain and humiliation caused by the break with Nadezhda Filaretovna von Meck. All that Tchaikovsky had brooded over ripened and poured into a confession of his soul in his last letter to Vladislav Pakhulsky.

PETER TCHAIKOVSKY TO VLADISLAV PAKHULSKY

Moscow, June 6, 1891

Dear Vladislav Albertovich:

Have just received your letter. I truly believe that Nadezhda Filaretovna is sick, weak, nervously upset, and cannot write to me as before. And not for anything in the world would I want her to suffer over me. I am grieved, perplexed and—I tell you frankly—deeply hurt, not because she doesn't write to me, but because she has entirely ceased to be interested in me. Had she truly desired that I keep regular correspondence with her, would it not have been entirely possible for you and Julia Karlovna to serve as steady mediators between us? But not once has she charged either of you to ask me to inform her about how I am or about what has happened to me. I have attempted through you to establish proper written communication with Nadezhda Filaretovna but every letter of yours has been merely a courteous acknowledgement of my efforts to retain, at least to some extent, a shadow of the past. You are no doubt aware that last September Nadezhda Filaretovna informed me that, having come to ruin, she could no longer render to me her material support. My answer to her is probably also known to you. It was my wish, my need that my relations with Nadezhda Filaretovna not change at all, simply because I had ceased to receive her money. To my regret, this turned out to be impossible in consequence of her quite apparent coolness to me. As a result, I stopped writing to Nadezhda Filaretovna and broke off almost all communication with her after I was deprived of her money. This situation humiliates me in my own eyes, making the remembrance that I had accepted her money intolerable. It constantly preys upon me and burdens me beyond measure. Last autumn in the country I reread all her old letters to me. Neither illness, nor misfortune, nor material difficulties could—so it seemed to me—change the sentiments which were uttered in those letters. And yet they did change. Perhaps for this reason alone, namely, that I have never known Nadezhda Filaretovna personally, she had seemed to me an ideal human being. I could not imaging fickleness in such a demigoddess; it seemed to me that the globe could sooner shatter into little pieces than Nadezhda Filaretovna's feelings change towards me. But the latter has happened, and it has turned upside down all my views about people and my faith in the best of them; it disturbs my peace and poisons that share of happiness allotted to me by fate. Still, apart from all this, N. F. has dealt with me most brutally. I have never felt as humiliated or hurt in my pride as now. And hardest of all to bear is the fact that, in view of the complete deterioration of her health, I am unable to express to her all that torments me, for fear of distressing and upsetting her.

There is no chance for me to have my say—yet only this would relieve me. But enough about this. Probably I will regret that I written all of the above,—but I needed at least to vent the bitterness gathering in my heart to someone.

Of course, not a word to Nadezhda Filaretovna about this.

If she wishes to know what I am doing, tell her that I happily returned from America, settled in the village of Maidanovo, and am at work. I am fine.

Do not answer this letter.

P. Tchaikovsky

My regards to Julia Karlovna.

This wound stayed forever with him, and on his deathbed, in the presence of his relatives, he repeated Nadezhda Filaretovna's name.

PETER TCHAIKOVSKY TO ALEXANDER ZILOTY[39]

City of Klin, Maidanovo, June 11, 1891

Golubchik Sasha,

For a long time I've intended to write to you but did not know your precise address. It's regrettable that we couldn't see each other and verbally discuss your affairs. But God willing, we will see each other in the early autumn. For the time being, rest and work. I wanted to tell you the following. Seryozha wrote you the truth: I am truly glad that you left the Conservatory. If you recall, I never approved of your move to Moscow, believing that at your age and with your great, virtuosic talent, you ought not to stay in one place but travel all around and perform. You have too many gifts for a brilliant, virtuosic career to cloister yourself in Moscow and spend your life sinking down into petty conservatory squabbles. For Taneyev, that authentic philosopher, who was created to work at a desk and who, through the grace of nature, has the ability to ascend high into the clouds, far above the cares of human life—for him, I would not advise a move away from Moscow. But you should positively not stay there. You waste your energy on a pack of trifles; one could fall apart and decline, by continuing to struggle against the petty tyranny of Safonov, the guile of Inspector Gubert, and similar nonsense. Let them stay in Moscow and fiddle about in their ant-hill—but you, the eagle, fly somewhat farther on, like a majestic, migratory bird. But I've fallen into high style. Speaking bluntly, you should go somewhat farther away and perform as much as possible. In my view, it would be good for you to go to America, not for one month, but for a whole year, perhaps for two. Nowhere but in America can a person (especially one of your fraternity—pianists) perform so often and earn so much money. In the first place, piano manufacturers are at sword's edge between themselves and pay pianists handsomely to woo them to their firms. Secondly, the need for talented virtuosos is tremendous, for there are a huge number of cities; concerts are held everywhere, and everyone is well-paid. Your acquaintance from Weimar, Adele Aus der Ohe, came to New York four years ago quite unknown and scored a success with the Philharmonic Society; since then she is always on the move all over America and has already managed to acquire a large fortune. What an energetic, pulsating and varied life it is for a young man! As I have a lot of friends and connections in America now, I would of course help you with your first steps; after that everything will be plain sailing. But if for now, i.e., for instance, in September, you don't want to go to America, why not travel a bit through Europe during the next season? In that case, of course, you can hardly do without Wolff. But could not Wolff be bribed? However, we will discuss all these details later verbally. As a traveling virtuoso you have one strike against you: you are married. But first, Vera is so nice, bold, and firm that she could go with you (the children you could leave with grandma) and second, this strike is at the same time a surprisingly favorable circumstance. Thanks to it you are provided for and at the beginning will not have to look for money, but only for the opportunity to play in public. So, after considering everything, I find that you should be glad to leave the Conservatory and starting in autumn you must give concerts, either in Europe or in America.

All in all I am very satisfied with my voyage, although I felt homesick while overseas and craved to be home with all my mind and heart. I am very glad to be back but recall by great success and the cordiality, hospitality, delightful welcome given to me in America with pleasure. Now after my week-long stay in Petersburg and a similar one in Moscow (where I met N. S. Zverev, Arensky, Remisov, and Kashkin) I've settled down in Maidanovo to work intensely, i.e., to compose the ballet and opera, orchestrate them and the symphonic fantasy *Voevoda*, rework the sextet, etc., etc. I received in Moscow two pages of the score of *The Tempest*, which you had sent to me. On those two pages, to my surprise, I found a great number of bad mistakes. How that came about—I can't understand. Meanwhile it turns out that you ordered it printed. After this shock I demanded the entire score, which I will look over now. Besides errors, of which I find only a few on the remaining pages, I am making corrections to the signs *p, f, cresc.*, etc., and adding metronome markings. Only after that will I send it to press. I also took four-hand dances from *Voevoda* and *Sleeping Beauty* to look over. Unfortunately I have no one with whom to play the latter. But so far the arrangement seems to be quite playable. Is it corrected well? It is very possible that, amidst the excitement connected with exams and the quarrel, you had no chance to give yourself over in full measure to the dull and laborious process of proofreading. But I am ashamed when I think what a burden you took on with the proofreading of my works and I don't wonder at all if by the end of the school year your energy in finding errors has been slightly weakened. No matter what the cost, Peter Ivanovich must obtain a proofreading specialist from Germany. Now that you are leaving, one is needed more than ever.

Now good-bye, dear Sasha! Forgive me, that I didn't write you from America—I really had no time for correspondence. A thousand kind words to Vera, whose hand I kiss.

Yours,
Tchaikovsky

MARY RENO TO PETER TCHAIKOVSKY

New York, June 28, 1891

Dear Maestro!

As soon as I received your first letter I planned to write you to thank you for those dear and kind lines.[40] Everyone in my family asks me to tell you that we've never stopped thinking of you. But at the moment that I was going to express all our sentiments in a letter, words seemed so cold that I decided not to send it. I must improve my French, so that it will be easier for me. If you wish, I will write next time in English. Don't laugh: I have started learning Russian, but it is very difficult,—in any case, I won't stop studying it.

Your letter from Russia, received yesterday, utterly fascinated me, and I can share the pleasure which you feel at being in your homeland.

You must know, dear Maestro, that the passion of your patriotism permeates all your works and ennobles them. I have lately scanned through (and studied a little) your marvelous Overture-Fantasy [*Hamlet*], Op. 67 once again. This is a magnificent work indeed if we could only see you conducting it! All your nature is mirrored in each of your compositions, and, consequently, all are authentic.

When will we be allowed to see you in New York? All of us hope it will be soon! This year we will not go to Europe. My husband and all my children send to you fond regards. We would be happy to have news of you from time to time and hope that you are well and can work in peace.

Accept, my dear "son-in-law," assurances of my sincere friendship.

Faithfully yours,
Mary Reno

ADELE AUS DER OHE TO PETER TCHAIKOVSKY

Celendorf, near Berlin, July 16, 1891

Most respected Maestro!

Now I am learning your Second concerto as well to add it to my repertoire. Did you not say, when I had the honour and the pleasure to meet with you in New York, that it would be desirable to emphasize some little nuances? Could I ask you to be so kind as to show them to me later, before I play it in public? For I would like to perform this concerto as close to your conception as possible. In early June, while still in New York, I sent with you letters for Messrs. Safonov, Auer, and Peterssen; and from the latter two I have already received answers. Nothing is definite, but I have not forsaken the goal of earning the right to appear in Russia, hopefully, along with your concerto, the performing of which under your direction is one of my most cherished memories!

By the way, Mr. Peterssen wrote me that he left Bekker's firm but will continue his membership in the Imperial Russian Musical Society.

I hope, you have pleasant memories of your trip to America!

The best regards from my sister and me and my deepest respect to you.

Truly yours,
Adele Aus der Ohe

Soon after Tchaikovsky's return to Russia, serious negotiations concerning a new tour to America were resumed.

PETER TCHAIKOVSKY TO JAKOV KALISHEVSKY[41]

City of Klin, village of Maidanovo, June 20, 1891

Dear Jakov Stepanovich!

You have read my mind. For a long while I myself meant to talk with you about a visit to America. But the matter was not pressing and I postponed writing to you due to a great deal of urgent proofreading work.

Here is the matter.

I am invited to come to America for a long series of concerts of Russian music. The head of the organization which is inviting me is a certain Mr. Carnegie, a very rich music lover. Two years ago he visited Russia and was greatly impressed by Russian sacred singing. He asked me to collect information on whether or not I will be able for my next visit to bring a choir, small in number but of superb quality, so that this chorus would sing sacred works and also folk songs, if possible, in my Russian concerts. I instantly thought about you and decided to make you this offer. It's occurred to me that you are probably bound up by some obligation with the Sofiysky cathedral and can't leave with a chorus for long. However, if this trip comes about, you would have to devote several months to it. Apparently, it is possible, and I am awfully glad of it. Now be so kind as to answer, right away, the following questions:

1. What sort of chorus could you recruit that would be small but very good? It's inconvenient for a large one to move from place to place. Is it possible to assemble one with no more than 24 people; or even less?

2. At what time can you make this trip? In New York they would like me to come next January, but I would like to stay in Russia this winter and prefer to go either in the fall of 1892 or January of 1893. However, if they insist very much, I may perhaps decide to go to America with you, even next January (1892). It would be of interest to know when you would like to go overseas.

3. Along with Bortniansky and all the other foremost sacred composers can you include in your repertoire a few folk songs as well?

4. How long can Grisha and his marvelous voice endure yet?

Upon receiving answers to these questions I will write to America that I've chosen a chorus and precentor and then will ask them to notify me on what terms they can offer. Then I will write you again. But in early autumn I hope to be in Kiev; we will have much to talk about.

My regards to your wife, the whole chorus, and a hug to Grisha. I wait for the answer.

Yours faithfully,
P. Tchaikovsky

Please, don't tell anybody about this matter yet. Where should I address letters to you?

WALTER DAMROSCH TO PETER TCHAIKOVSKY

Bayreuth, July 4, 1891

Most respected Mr. Tchaikovsky,

We earnestly desire to have you in America for the next winter. Would this be possible? And if it would work out,— with a Russian church choir. Along with your own compositions you might also conduct works of other Russian composers too. The beautiful days of last May still ring within me. I cannot forget how much you contributed to the success.

If you are able to come in early or middle February, kindly drop me a few lines, and Mr. Reno too. Your terms, etc. I have already invited little Conius and also Brodsky, your friend and admirer.

With fond greetings,
Another of your admirers,
Walter Damrosch

PETER TCHAIKOVSKY TO WALTER DAMROSCH

City of Klin, near Moscow, July 7, 1891

Dear highly respected friend,

I've just received your friendly note. The letter was awaiting me for I've just come back today from a short trip. I hope that my answer can still reach you in Bayreuth.

I am prepared to go to America again, next February, and very glad of it. I've already gathered together a superb church choir (thirty men and boys) and the conductor of the choir, a Mr. Kalishevsky from Kiev, writes me that he is ready to go with me at any time. Excuse me for continuing in French; it's too difficult for me to write in German.

To finish with this matter, it's necessary for me to know the precise sum that they will offer Mr. Kalishevsky. Consider, my friend, that for bringing a whole chorus society to America for several weeks—the cost is very dear! It's necessary to fix costs for the trip and other expenses and also the sum which can be proposed to Mr. Kalishevsky as payment for his and his choir's efforts.

So, I will wait until Mr. Reno reflects a bit, calculates what they will be able to offer Kalishevsky, fixes the sum that he can propose, and lets me know. It seems you have offered to convey my terms to Mr. Reno. I am not too interested but, all the same, I would not mind earning some money in America. I truly don't know what I can demand and would prefer that Mr. Reno propose what could be given to us.

You will not believe how happy and grateful I am to you for engaging little Conius. As for Brodsky, who is one of my best friends and is considered to be an excellent artist,—I will gladly keep it in mind to see him in New York.

Where is the supremely attractive Mrs. Damrosch? I send her my heartiest regards. I embrace you, my good, dear friend!

Respectfully yours,
P. Tchaikovsky

By all means, I will conduct many other Russian things, besides my own compositions.

PETER TCHAIKOVSKY TO VLADIMIR NAPRAVNIK

City of Klin, village of Maidanovo, July 25, 1891

My friend Volodia,

You are awfully miserly with letters and adhere too stubbornly to the system of only answering mine. But, my dear sir, I am burdened with work and can only write by taking time off from my labor, while you are certainly not impressing the inhabitants of Gugenburg, Meriful, Sillamiag, etc. from dawn to dusk with your inconceivably great talent for concert accompanying. You should now and then think of the grey old man who shows a keen interest in everything that concerns the Napravniks and craves for news about them. And yet you are the nicest human being and I love you very much.

I am sitting in my burrow working hard, but, it seems, not very successfully. More and more I ask myself whether I've exhausted my inspiration and should be granted a full respite from composition. How often I've noticed that I've fallen into repeating myself. The painful minutes of doubts within myself!!! Be that as it may, I've made a rough version of the ballet, and am writing the opera now in hopes of finishing it in late August. Then I will go to rest in Kamenka. I was in Petersburg in late June; in early July I met frequently with Sania Litke. I am in correspondence about my invitation to visit America again in January. I will go only in the case of especially advantageous terms. I have for some reason no desire to go anywhere and have become old and sluggish.

Please, dear Volodechka, tell me about your dad and whether he is well or still very upset by the nasty thing that happened with the Don Juan. This story truly disturbed me. Write about Mama and all of you. Give my fondest greetings to your parents, sisters, and Kotia.

LEON MARGULIS[42] TO PETER TCHAIKOVSKY

New York, August 25, 1891

Dear Mr. Tchaikovsky,

Concerning the engagement of the chorus, a matter you bring up in your most cordial letter of July 19 to Mrs. Reno, Mr. Reno asks me to inform you that he has conveyed to Mr. Carnegie all of your propositions, in so far as they pertain to the principal amount. For the present Carnegie is in Scotland. We will let you know immediately upon receipt of his answer.

At that time the matter of your invitation can be settled. In the meantime accept my fondest regards.

Yours faithfully,
Leon Margulis

On September 6, 1891 Tchaikovsky received a letter from Jurgenson which included a telegram from Morris Reno, inviting Tchaikovsky to visit America again for two months to conduct a series of concerts for the fee of $4000. On the reverse side of this telegram Jurgenson wrote a note: "How do you like him? I hope you will not take less than $1000 for each concert? Then buy an estate for the money!"

PETER TCHAIKOVSKY TO PETER JURGENSON

Maidanovo, September 7, 1891

After having an engagement last season to conduct four concerts in America, a trifling thing (for $2500), after having a truly great success there, I find Mr. Reno's present proposal almost insolent. Therefore I will reply insolently too. Be kind enough to send the following telegram right away: "New York, 154 West 73 Street, Morris Reno. Non. Tchaikovsky." For my part I don't want to insist upon any conditions, for this year I prefer not to go to America at all. The word "Non" is sufficient for him to realize the impropriety of his propositions. Please, send the telegram immediately. I don't want to write, for I am afraid of using strong words. Please, send the attached message to Gesenklever's store and ask him to send here all the things marked on the list. Laroche will be staying here with me for a long time and we would like to play four-hand [music].

Also, send me the score of Beethoven's B-flat Major Fourth Symphony. I will buy it, but four-hand things I take on loan.

A full tragedy is occurring here apropos of my watch. The pilferer was found and has confessed, but it's now three weeks and we still can't obtain from him where the watch is. One by one, a great number of innocent people were arrested. Finally the affair has now entered a new phase. The thief indicates and the circumstances confirm, that the watch is hidden at the Novikov's (mother and son). All of Klin and all the neighbouring villages talk only of this shady and queer business. As to the Novikovs—don't tell a soul.

I am not well today. I embrace you.

P. Tchaikovsky

The investigation into the matter of my watch is costing me a lot of money. In general, I can relate a lot of interesting things about this affair. When is Osip Ivanovich going to come to you? I have sent him a business letter and am afraid that it will not reach him.

Thus the conversation about the Tchaikovsky's new tour to America led to nothing. However it was resumed, this time thanks to Hermann Wolff. On October 10, 1891 Tchaikovsky received a letter from Berlin:

Dear friend,

I offer you a tour to America. This country is now familiar to you, and you must know, how much they adore you there.

Would you like to conduct twenty-five concerts (or fewer if that is too many) in April or May using the best orchestras? At each concert you will conduct only a few numbers (from your works).

What royalties should I request? I expect your answer at once—the matter is urgent.

I wait for your letter and shake your hand as a friend.

Hermann Wolff

The entrepreneur is in Berlin now. Reno should have written you already about these concerts. There is no need for you to write Reno. I have been entrusted with this affair.

PETER TCHAIKOVSKY TO PETER JURGENSON

Maidanovo, Octover 8, 1891

Listen to this. In view of the many demands for *Hamlet,* please lithograph the parts just as they are. I only ask that it be marked if old pieces were adapted from some other work. Then a few good examples of new music—[the music] for the melodrama, for the ghost's appearance, the march, and even, if you like, the overture—could be published in score format, if it is indicated that this overture is a réduction facilité of the large overture. However we can discuss all of this very soon. If America gives me the 20,000 roubles I demand and I spend, presumably, even half of it for travel, 10,000 roubles would still remain. This would be quite good for my heirs.

Good-bye.

Yours,
Tchaikovsky

PETER TCHAIKOVSKY TO PETER JURGENSON

Maidanovo, October 13, 1891

Dear Friend!

Immediately wire the following:
"Reno, New York
Can't accept less then $12,000, letter follows.
P. Tchaikovsky"
Good-bye!

P. Tchaikovsky

PETER TCHAIKOVSKY TO VLADIMIR DAVIDOV

Maidanovo, October 12, 1891

For God's sake forgive me, my idol, my darling, that I have thought so little about your financial needs. However, even before I received the letter from Modest today, in which he reminded me to send money to you, I had already entrusted Laroche with handing over to you 50 roubles in the meantime. Early next month I can spare you a bit more, but I will be especially rich before Christmas, when I receive a considerable sum from theaters in both capitals. For God's sake ask me for money any time you need it, not to mention the budgetary 50 roubles a month which are your right to demand. I long to see you and have often thought to make a short trip to Peter[sburg] for this purpose, but common sense has compelled me to stay at home and work. My peregrinations will begin soon and I am at a loss as to when I can complete the instrumentation of both large scores! From October 15 till November 7 I will be in Moscow, next in Peter[sburg] and Revel, then in Hamburg and Prague, after that, in Holland, then perhaps in Paris, and in spring perhaps in America. I have serious proposals to spend April and May in New York, etc. I asked for $12,000 (20,000 roubles). If they give it, I'll go. They offered me twenty concerts. So you see, I must use every spare minute to work. The instrumentation of the opera is progressing, but not very quickly. This one-act opera is enormous and demands great attention throughout. I will not see you before November!!! I kiss you, my angel!

Yours,
P. Tchaikovsky

Please, if you need more money now, let me know. I am sending not 50, but 60 roubles.

PETER TCHAIKOVSKY TO KONSTANTIN ROMANOV

Moscow, October 31, 1891

Your Majesty,

It is difficult to express how glad and how touched I was by your dear note. Of course, in the depths of my soul I sensed that you hadn't forgotten me,—but it is so pleasant to have the material evidence showing that, along with such intricate and diverse occupations and while still under the influence of heavy family grief, you could spare a part of your time to remember me. For some time I've not had the good fortune to see you but from various sources I have always kept track of what has happened to you, have rejoiced at your delights and mourned over your sorrows. On the evening of September 15 I actually saw you at the Nikolayevskaya railroad station in Klin but I did not come up to you, fearing my greeting would be ill-timed in the midst of those circumstances which had placed you on your way from Ilyinskoe. Your niece's death affected me deeply. Without exaggeration I can say that I cried for her as if I'd known her intimately and well. I can imagine how painful it was for you! As one grows old, one begins to regard every death either with indifference or a calm consciousness of the inevitable fact of death; but the deaths of very young people, especially of those for whom circumstances promised happiness, have always depressed me.

Since I saw Your Majesty the last time, I managed to go to America. This trip leaves me with no pleasant reminiscences. The day before my departure from Le Havre I received news about my sister's death and under this oppressive influence experienced the ocean, which, for all its ineffable beauty, has not the virtue to dispel sorrow. On the contrary, the ocean merely intensified it. In America they gave me an exceedingly warm welcome. I saw a host of interesting, original, and beautiful things there (Niagara Falls, for instance), but I was so fiercely, inexpressibly, painfully homesick, and so longed to be back with every vessel of my inner being, that my entire month-long stay there was true misery. But then, I believe, despite everything I was so much the happier when I returned to Russia and saw all those who are dear to me. I spent all summer in the country working. Yesterday I completed the one-act opera *Iolanthe* (*King René's Daughter*) and the ballet *Nutcracker* (*Cassenoisette*). At present I am in Moscow in order to attend the rehearsals for *The Queen of Spades,* which will be given here for the first time, soon after November 1.

It was quite pleasant to make Fet's[43] acquaintance. Afanasy Afanasyevich touched me with his friendly welcome. Judging by his memoirs, published in the *Russian Herald,* I'd thought that his conversation would not be particularly interesting. On the contrary, he proved to be an extraordinarily pleasing conversationalist, full of originality and humor. If you could see, Your Majesty, how charming his summer residence is! What a house, what a park, what a cozy refuge for the aging poet! Unfortunately, as Maria Petrovna told me, our poet doesn't enjoy the pleasure of living in these poetic surroundings at all. He stays at home without going out, dictates the translation of Martial or his own verses, quarrels with the young lady who takes down his dictations, and goes not further than his balcony. He recited to me many of his new verses, and I was astonished at how young and fresh his muse still is. We both regretted that circumstances have prevented Your Majesty from devoting yourself to poetic work. If you could only allow yourself to take a rest in the summer by living somewhere in solitude! But alas!—this, too, is impossible.

After the first performance of *The Queen of Spades* I will go to the country and devote myself to the opera's instrumentation. In mid-December I will be in Petersburg, where I am invited to conduct a concert of the Russian Musical Society. I hope I will manage to see Your Majesty and the Grand Princess. Next I am obliged to travel to Hamburg and Prague for productions of my operas. In April I am

invited to go to America, but it seems to me that a quiet
stay in the country, where I could work, would be prefera-
ble to the material advantages associated with the trip.
Upon finishing my present compositions I want very much
to abandon the writing of operas and ballets, to work for a
while in the symphonic field. One often arrives at the
thought that perhaps it is time to completely close up shop.
The point is that a composer, once he's achieved success
and recognition of his merits, becomes a hindrance for
young composers who seek the opportunity to stage their
works. There was a time, when no one wanted to know of
me; without the Grand Duke's (your father's) patronage, no
operas of mine would have been accepted for the stage.
Now they spoil and encourage me in every possible way. It
is very pleasing but do I perhaps prevent young composers
from reaching the stage? This frequently bothers and tortures me.

I humbly beg Your Majesty to extend my fervent greetings to the Great Duchess and once again thank you from
the depths of my soul, for granting me the honor of being
your obedient servant.

P. Tchaikovsky

LEON MARGULIS TO PETER TCHAIKOVSKY

New York, November 13, 1891

My dear Mr. Tchaikovsky:

Your highly esteemed letter of October 25 came to me
and I relayed its content to Mr. Reno. It is true that your
demand for $12,000 seemed excessive to us but we took it
as a declination to make the trip to our country. By the way
the proposal of $4000 was made by neither Mr. Reno nor
the Music Hall Company but by the impresario Mr. D.
Blakely who also presumably wrote to Wolff in Berlin. He
asked that Mr. Reno make you an offer. My father-in-law
even remarked to Mr. Blakely that $4000 was rather scant

for you and that you should be offered at least a guaranteed minimum of $5000 for two months. Even the latter is little in comparison with that sum which you received for the Musical Festival but that was a special event—the inauguration of the edifice, built by a multimillionaire who would have spent any amount to make the event as brilliant as possible. But when it is a matter of inviting an artist for a tour and a certain profit must be considered, then it is all clear and simple: a definite limit can't be exceeded without the risk of incurring losses.

The musical season in the Music Hall began today with the first concert, a matinee, of the Symphony Society and Brodsky's debut in New York. He had a great success with the Brahms concerto. Your Hamlet was performed, also with great success. By the way no concert can go by without the playing of one of your works.

I must hurry to end this letter for I am being disturbed every minute. Mrs. Reno however will have the pleasure to write you one of these days. We are all delighted with your letters. I forgot to add that Mr. Reno would make you a proposal on his own but prefers to wait for the next season since too many concerts are already arranged for the current season. Accept, dear Sir, fondest regards from my wife, Mr. Reno, Alice, and from all my remaining family.

Faithfully yours,
Leon Margulis

PETER TCHAIKOVSKY TO WILLIAM VON SACHS

Paris, January 17, 1892

My dear friend,

Your letter just reached me; it traveled much before catching me. How nice of you that you didn't forget about me! You deeply touched me, and can be certain I extend to you the same cordial sentiments which permeate your letter. Accept from me a thousand wishes for prosperity and happiness on the occasion of the coming New Year. I will be very glad to meet you in Europe and if you let me know where you are going to spend the summer, it is highly probable I will be able to see you and shake hands with you. As for my return to America—I doubt the chance will come to me. Despite my sincere desire to see again the country where I was so well received,—it demands too much time, effort, and fatigue. One must have a lot of money and a great deal of leisure to allow himself this pleasure; I have neither. It is true, Mr. Reno has made me a proposal, but on such poor conditions that I could take it for a bad joke, especially after the host of compliments lavished upon me to excess during my stay in New York! My God, how many grandiose projects, how many promises and ardent requests, how much generosity and exalted enthusiasm! And all this ended in an incomprehensible pettiness. It appears, speaking seriously, that my musical personality offers insignificant interest for America, which surprises me much less than do the exaggerated praises, which were lavished upon me when I was there.

Good-bye, dear, kind friend.

Yours,
P. Tchaikovsky

Thus the second round of negotiations for a new visit to America produced nothing except mutual discontent. Yet this idea took deep root on both sides of the Atlantic. As we will see, various attempts towards resolution of the matter were made.

In spite of his wounded feelings and the failure of his dream to earn money in America, Tchaikovsky viewed the country as a promised land for musicians. He tried to find ways there for his friends, and with intense sincerity recommended that they sail across the ocean. His two friends Julius Conius and Adolf Brodsky were about to start their careers overseas, and Tchaikovsky deeply cared about how things would go for them. Conius, the new assistant concertmaster in the New York Symphony Society Orchestra, was already preparing for the journey overseas. To gather money for this trip Tchaikovsky helped Conius to arrange a special concert, in which, besides Conius, the following friends of the composer also participated: the composer Taneev, the cellist Brandukov, and the contralto Lavrovskaya. Several of Tchaikovsky's works were performed. The composer himself attended the concert.

PETER TCHAIKOVSKY TO PETER JURGENSON

Maidanovo, September 22, 1891

Dear friend,

I really want to help Conius, at least a bit, with raising [money]. Tickets are to be sold at your place. If you see that receipts are poor, please, take for me 15–20 tickets and hand them out at your office to whomever you want in general; of course, say nothing to Conius.

I will come Sunday morning, and see you at the concert.

Yours,
P. Tchaikovsky

My regards to all.

The conductor of the Russian Symphony Orchestra in New York (since 1903), Modest Altschuler, recalls:

(From Musical America, April 25, 1947)

Julius Conius, a talented young violinst of French extraction, was befriended by Tchaikovsky when the composer came to the United States. Arrangements were made to have Walter Damrosch engage him as second concertmaster for his new orchestra at Carnegie Hall. We had a benefit concert to raise money for his journey. Among the general run of moneyless, ill-clad, badly groomed, ill-fed, happy-go-lucky students of the conservatory, Conius, in contrast, was always immaculately dressed with innate Gallic taste.

His concert was a big event. I went for a more personal

reason than the rest. My brother Jacob was already in the United States, a member of the Damrosch New York Symphony, and I wanted Conius to convey certain information to him. The program of the evening contained Tchaikovsky's Trio played by Conius, cellist Brandukov and Taneyev. The great contralto Lavrovskaya sang "At the Ball" and shorter numbers were sandwiched in. Among these, to our astonishment, Tchaikovsky had allowed his favorite to put in the Andante Cantabile from the First string quartet in an arrangement Conius made for violin and piano! How the composer could sit there and listen to his creation minus the glorious tonal web of the three other instruments replaced by the tinkling sound of the piano, the students could not understand. . . .

But it was one of Tchaikovsky's virtues to treat others. Tchaikovsky provided Conius with the following letter:

PETER TCHAIKOVSKY TO ADOLF BRODSKY

Moscow, September 30, 1891

Dear Adolf and dear, sweet Anna Lvovna,

I entrust to your favorable attention my dear and likable friend Julius Conius. I am convinced that you both will come to love and cherish him.

Adolf, I embrace you hard and kiss Anna Lvovna's hand!

P. Tchaikovsky

Adolf Brodsky, who was to become concertmaster of the New York Symphony Society Orchestra and stand partner of Julius Conius, had been an old friend of Tchaikovsky's since their days of working together as professors at the Moscow conservatory. In 1888 they met each other in Leipzig, at a time when Brodsky taught in its conservatory and was leader of a string quartet widely known in Europe. Brodsky was the first performer of Tchaikovsky's Violin Concerto and recipient of its dedications. "Brodsky is one of the most likable

men that I have ever encountered . . . he is a beautiful artist and
quartet performer, the most perfect among all whom I have heard,"
wrote Tchaikovsky in one letter.

PETER TCHAIKOVSKY TO JULIUS CONIUS

Maidanovo, November 23, 1891

Julik, my dear,

At last I've received direct news from you. Frankly speaking, it hurt me a bit that you sent me no news right when
you arrived,—as indeed you had promised, and I was seriously anxious about you till I met the professor of music
theory, George Eduardovich and was told that you had
nearly reached your destination. Goodness, it all seems so
long ago: your playing my trio, our seeing each other on
the next day for the last time, my following your trip in my
thoughts. Since then I've managed to work a great deal,
stay in Moscow for a few weeks, stage *Queen of Spades*
(which practically failed), and conduct Ziloty's concert,
where I directed my new symphonic work *Voevoda*, which
came out so foul that the next day I tore it to shreds. Indeed what things have not changed since then??? Do you
know, I've begun to age quickly, to tire of life, to long quite
often for peace and rest from all the bustle, excitements,
disappointments, etc., etc. But it's all nonsense. An oldtimer
naturally has to think of that vile hole nearby which is
called a grave—but a young man should look boldly and
cheerfully to the future. Judging by the tone of your letter
I see that you've not yielded to spleen. If you don't enjoy
the life in the new place, then you don't suffer either. I am
awfully glad that you became friends with Brodsky (d, not t
as you wrote). He is a nice person in the full sense of the
word and the only Jew entirely free from the faults that are
peculiar to this gifted tribe. And his wife is simply charming! But for them, I would be suffering for you. How it
pleased me that in praising Brodsky's talent you confessed

your envy. This kind of envy is nothing else but a striving for perfection; this is a sign that you will not come to a halt. I will not be in America in the spring. For two months and 25 concerts they offered me such a miserable pittance that it would have made me resentful—but let it pass! They did not give me my price. And I am glad, for it will be a chance to stay quietly at home and work. As for you—I hope to see you here in summer. I embrace you hard, dear creature.

Yours,
P. Tchaikovsky

A thousand kind words to Brodsky.

PETER TCHAIKOVSKY TO ADOLF BRODSKY

Maidanovo, October 19, 1891

Dear friend Adolf,

Indeed I've not forgotten you—a strange thought!—and have lately attempted many times to write to you. But for the life of me I could not find your summer address among old letters. I particularly wanted to wish you and Anna Lvovna happiness in your new home and good luck in your new field of work. At the bottom of your heart you could not doubt my most sincere friendship and concern for you, and therefore I was actually somewhat hurt by your thinking that I could forget you. I assure you that I am quite faithful and firm in my conviction that I have always loved you very much, and, in consequence of particular circumstances, after making the acquaintance of your wife, after Leipzig, have grown to love you even more. Lately I have more than once grieved over the thought that fate brings people together, arranges intimacies between them, and then parts them again for a few years or more so that a sense of oblivion becomes possible! No, dearest, I truly did not forget either you or the most charming Anna Lvovna; I

often think of you and sincerely miss you. At this moment I
can vividly see you on board the *Fürst Bismarck,* which is so
familiar to me. Later I will vividly picture you in my mind
amidst New York surroundings. Long ago I learned from
Damrosch about your engagement and approved of your
decision to move to America. I am certain that you will settle down perfectly well there and be satisfied in all respects.
But at first will you not long a bit for your cozy nest in
Leipzig? It's quite possible,—but time will cure all that, and
in the end I see only the best in your resolve to go across
the ocean.

I have nothing particularly new to say about myself. I
work as hard as before. During the current season I must
orchestrate two large scores, be in Hamburg and Prague
for opera productions, give concerts in Holland and
France, and conduct many concerts in various parts of Russia. I am invited to America for the spring,—but it seems
that this won't take place. I am offered too scanty a fee,
one which will hardly reimburse the fare. I asked for three
times as much but most likely they will not agree, which will
nor surprise or offend me at all.

I will try to help with the concerto parts. I have a favor
of the same kind to ask of you. I left, i.e., I was not given
back, the parts to the Third Suite, which I performed in
New York, because the entire orchestra and the manager of
sheet music departed for a music festival. Meanwhile I desperately need them for a new edition. I wrote Reno and his
son-in-law about these parts in summer—but have not received them. For goodness' sake make sure that they are
found and sent to Jurgenson in Moscow.

Golubchik, I recommend to you your stand partner, Conius. He is not only a talented and sensible youth but a
young man excellent in all respects, who comes from an
unusually talented and marvelous family. Lately I've come
to love him very much since growing close to him in Paris
and was awfully glad for him when I learned of your moving to America. It will be the greatest happiness for him to

find in an alien land such good people and compatriots, as yourself and Anna Lvovna. I beg both of you to care for this dear young fellow, who is entirely worthy of your sympathy.

Please, give my deepest respects to Damrosch and his wife, the Renos and the host of all my friends in New York, among whom you live and work. I keep the warmest reminiscences of New York and of the cordiality of its natives. Americans are an unusually appealing, straightforward, simple, and sincere people. Remind Conius that he promised to write me.

I embrace you hard, my dear friend Adolf. I kiss Anna Lvovna's hand. God willing, in summer I will manage to visit you.

Yours,
P. Tchaikovsky

Musical Courier, November 18, 1891
First Symphony Society concert

The first concert of the Symphony Society and the initial concert of the new Music Hall, Fifty-seventh street and Seventh avenue, took place last Saturday evening, preceded by the usual rehearsal Friday afternoon. The program was as follows: Beethoven—Symphony No. 7 in A, Brahms—Concerto for Violin and Orchestra, Tchaikovsky—"Hamlet," Fantasy-Overture, Wagner—"Kaiser March."

The orchestra, which was greatly reinforced at the regular concert, played neither better nor worse than formerly. The same raggedness of attack, the same uncontrolled and overpowering sonority, and the same lack of light in details characterized the performance. Then, too, the woodwind in company with the brass choir was faulty in intonation, something that Mr. Damrosch did not seem to notice, and the Beethoven symphony was read with a wilful disregard of dynamics and even the original rhythmical intentions of the composer. The timpani was positively brutal at times. The redeeming feature of the evening was the superb violin playing of Mr. Adolph Brodsky, the newly imported concertmaster of the society, who gave a manly, musical and technically finished reading to Brahms' beautiful violin concerto in D, a work that exhibits its composer in the best light, for it is fecund as to motives, conceived in the loftiest musical vein, and the workmanship is solid and simple.

Mr. Brodsky, who is a long felt want supplied, for New York has hitherto had no great resident violin artists, covered himself with glory, and responded with the Adagio of the G-minor violin sonata of Bach. His influence will doubtless be felt in the orchestra, the personnel of which is strong, the new solo cellist, Anton Hekking, and Julius Conius, violinist, being worthy additions. The mystery will be if Mr. Damrosch with such an orchestral force and abundant rehearsals does not do strong work during the season. The MUSICAL COURIER hopes so.

Musical Courier, December 9, 1891

A new quartet club

A new string quartet club of such strength as the New York Symphony String Quartet, which had its first public hearing last Sunday afternoon in the Chamber Music Hall of the new Music Hall, cannot go without a passing word. The club is under the artistic leadership of Mr. Adolph Brodsky, its first violin, and the concertmaster of the Symphony Society Orchestra.

The second violin is Mr. Julius Conius, a French artist Mr. Damrosch especially engaged for the orchestra, to sit at the same desk with Mr. Brodsky. The viola is Jan Koert, a most excellent artist, and the cello is Anton Hekking, who is in addition to being a virtuoso on his instrument, also a fine chamber music performer. . . .

So for the third time in one year the Hamlet *Fantasy Overture by Tchaikovsky was performed in New York, this time by the New York*

Symphony Society Orchestra under Walter Damrosch, as part of the opening concert of the first season at the new Music Hall. In this same concert Tchaikovsky's two friends Brodsky and Conius performed for the first time with the orchestra. From then on Tchaikovsky's music continued to be heard often in this remarkable hall. Two weeks later the Second Symphony was performed; the Violin Concerto (with Brodsky as soloist) came next, followed by the Francesca da Rimini *Symphonic Fantasy, and others.*

Meanwhile in Maidanovo Tchaikovsky was finishing the work on the ballet Nutcracker *and the opera* Iolanthe; *simultaneously he was writing a new edition of his sextet and completing the instrumentation of the symphonic ballad* Voevoda.[44] *In the spring of 1892 Tchaikovsky moved to a new and final dwelling, a house he bought in the outskirts of Klin, which would become a museum after the composer's death. In the same spring the new, third round of negotiations over the engagement of Tchaikovsky to come to America began. This time he was asked to come to Chicago to participate in the World's Fair or "Columbian Exposition" of 1893.*

PETER TCHAIKOVSKY TO MIKHAIL IPPOLITOV-IVANOV [45]

Moscow, April 6, 1892

Dear Misha,

I came to Moscow just today and received your letter. I have much to do and can't write in detail—but I don't want to put off my answer. Some phrases in your letter anger and hurt me, for instance, the question: is it true that I forgot you and love you no longer? Do you mean to seriously confront me with this question? I thought you knew me better. I am not able to betray, to cool towards friends without motive, to forget them, etc. As to my scarce letters, this is quite understandable. I work like a slave and when I don't work, I travel and run about. Writing is difficult for me. Believe it or not,—I really think of you quite often and with all my heart long for dear Tiflis. Alas, everything can't happen as one would like it to. But I hope that I will manage to come this autumn to the banks of the Kura. Now I am in Moscow fulfilling my promise to conduct three operas: *Faust, Demon,* and *Onegin,* for Pryanishnikov. I made this promise, because in my presence Pryanishnikov and his fellowship, who I like very much, were insulted and wronged by Kiev's council. I wanted to help them with their new business as much as I could. It will be hard, unpleasant, even foolish (for what kind of opera conductor am I),—but nothing's to be done. I have completed the opera and the ballet. *Iolanthe* is being engraved. When it is set, I'll send it to you. I am not yet preparing for America but they have given me a proposal from Chicago for next summer. I don't know whether or not I'll accept the invitation. I am waiting for the agent who is coming to Moscow to discuss the matter.

Forgive, Misha, that I write so little,—I am very tired. A thousand kind words to Varvara Mikhailovna, Tata, Anna Mikhailovna, and all my friends. I will soon try to write to you again. Ask Kokodes why he didn't inform me about receiving the letter with enclosure.

Yours,
P. Tchaikovsky

I will be staying here until late April. I shall spend May in Klin. Anatoly's address is: Tobolsk. Governor's office.

PETER TCHAIKOVSKY TO THEODORE THOMAS

Klin, near Moscow, May 4, 1892

Dear Mr. Thomas:

I am aware that you recommended me to the board of the World Exhibition in Chicago. Thank you for that, I am very flattered, very proud of it,—but I hardly believe that it is possible. I can't come gratis, this is too great a burden, and they would like to pay only my travel expenses. Nevertheless I cordially thank you!

I have much to say to you,—but German is too difficult for me to write. I know how much you have done for me, or rather, for my music, in America. I beg you, dearest Sir and friend, do not doubt that I am truly grateful to you.

Truly yours,
P. Tchaikovsky

PETER TCHAIKOVSKY TO PETER JURGENSON

Klin, May 5, 1892

My dear one,

I am writing late in the night, long to sleep, and therefore will reply briefly, point by point:

1) Send me some vodka (this kind of vital fluid has cost me quite dearly) by freight train.

2) It's quite necessary that you send me the score of the Suite; it can't be printed without my checking.

3) I am awaiting the page from *Voevoda* and beg your pardon for my absent-mindedness.

4) Juferov has not sent me his opera and I have not been its subscriber (an odd question: it's the same as asking me whether or not I'd like to buy bull[. . .] and eat it). But I was invited to the Directorate in Petersburg two months ago or so, when Jurefov performed his opera, and gave this impudent fellow a good deal of unpleasantness. I've not read the advertisement.

5) I have written Crawford that I am much obliged for the honor but don't understand why I was called: if for the pleasure of attending the exhibition, I would avoid it, for I hate all exhibitions and the claustrophobia and fuss associated with them; if for the conducting, then I can't be satisfied with the fee for expenses, even less so because this expression is very elastic. I cannot present a bill to the exhibition which exceeds true expenses but I am not going to leave empty-handed either, for I value my time and labor highly. Consequently I'm demanding a fee of $10,000 for

the four-week stay in Chicago and my pledge to conduct
the Russian concerts. Whatever.

P. Tchaikovsky

PETER TCHAIKOVSKY TO PETER JURGENSON

Vishi, June 22, 1892

At last I have news of you. I sympathize with your suffering due to the Caucasian heat. What could be worse! It is
indescribably hot here too!

Be kind enough, golubchik, to write Thomas that if I do
cut back on the $10,000, it will only be by a little bit, pre-
cisely one-fifth. Less than $8,000 I will not accept. Why the
hell must I torture, suffer, constrain myself for no profit? I
am really capable of spending half of my fee right there,—
so at least the other half I'll bring with me. But if you find
it wiser to stay with 10,000,—so much the better. Write also
that it will be a great relief for me if you come with me.
However I don't doubt at all they will give neither 10,000
nor 8,000. And this will be the most pleasant solution for
me.

Thomas has written me, and I have answered him,—but
only his musical questions. He asked if I have a vocal work
(not an opera), and I pointed out the "Moscow" Cantata. If
the deal is made, then it will be necessary to provide a
translation.

Hope to see you in about three weeks.

Yours,
P. Tchaikovsky

*And again nothing resulted from the bargaining. Tchaikovsky did
not go to Chicago; the Russian concerts in the World's Fair were
conducted by Voitek Glavach. All the same the plan for another visit
to America was kept alive on both sides of the Atlantic Ocean. Were
it not for the composer's death during the following year, the visit
apparently might have taken place.*

PETER TCHAIKOVSKY TO JULIUS CONIUS

Klin, February 5, 1893

My dear Julik,

Yesterday evening I returned from a three-months' journey and among the letters found a most lovely one from you. How annoying it is that in the fall we missed each other! While in Tirole at Menter's I received your first long letter, in which you fully informed me about your plan to found a quartet and about something else. Apropos of this letter I wanted to tell you a great deal but since in a short time you had to leave for Russia, I decided that it was worthless to write and better to converse verbally in either Moscow or Klin. I came in sweet hopes of seeing and embracing you and suddenly found out from George that you had up and left. Soon after I went to Petersburg for the opera staging and then to various places abroad. As always I have not infrequently remembered your dear, roguish mug, but I have no time at all for detailed conversation. I write all this so that you would not interpret my long silence as a cooling towards you and would know that regardless of how lazy I am about letters and no matter how long I've kept you without them, there will always be a very snug and warm spot for you in my heart. But tell me, Julik, why in your last letter is there not the least hint of all the things that were included in the previous one? Why are you writing nothing these days about either the quartet or, most important, about your matrimonial plans? Indeed this is of capital interest. Or has all this vanished without a trace? Please, when you have time, answer for me all these questions.

Now I'll tell you something about myself. My new opera [*Iolanthe*] and ballet [*Nutcracker*] were given in Petersburg on December 6. The success was not absolute. The opera apparently had great appeal,—but the ballet, quite a bit

less. It proved indeed, despite its luxuriance, to be somewhat tedious. As usual, the newspapers scolded me harshly.
Following this, I was obliged to go to the stagings of this
same opera in Hamburg and Schwerin, which I nearly did,
except that in Berlin, I felt so tired, so incapable of suffering yet again, for two more times, the despair and tribula-
tions that torment the composer of a new opera as he is
tortured by the customary mayhem at rehearsals, that suddenly I resolved instead to set off for Switzerland and the
little town of France Montbeliard, where my governess re-
sides, a woman I have not seen for 44 years and to whom
I'd given my word to visit. This meeting gave me great
pleasure. From there I went to Paris, where I spent ten
very pleasant days incognito. I saw Ziloty and Delin—and
no one else, besides Makkar. Afterwards I had a big and
brilliant concert in Brussels, then again was in Paris and
this time made several necessary visits (I don't know
whether you are aware that I was elected Correspondent of
the Academy). From there went directly to Odessa (four
days). There I had three big concerts and a staging of
Queen of Spades. Finally, after staying in Odessa for two
weeks and becoming exhausted from the celebrations of
thereabouts, came home. But I shall not rest long. In a
week I conduct in Moscow, in the Music Society, for the
benefit of the Fund. Next I go to Kharkov, then to Petersburg, however soon I will reside at my place, and you can
write me here. In late May I will depart for the jubilee at
the University of Cambridge, on account of which (that is,
the jubilee) I was elected Doctor of Music and must conduct there and in London as well. But enough about myself.

A sad note resounds in your letter. Pour out your feelings on my friendly breast, dear Julik. Will you return to
Russia? When will we see each other? I probably will not go
to Chicago but, who knows, if they invite me to Music Hall
in the next winter for a decent fee, I might make the trip,

at least in order to embrace you and Brodsky. I've just seen Sapelnikov and Menter in Odessa. Do you know that in September I visited her in Itter? What a luxury is that place! And now with indescribable fondness I embrace you, my dear friend, and remain your faithful friend,

P. Tchaikovsky

Give my greetings to Brodsky, Anna Lvovna, and also to Damrosch.

This final period in Tchaikovsky's life was particularly full of emotional and nervous tensions. He traveled restlessly, and every time he was outside Russia he longed even more strongly for his homeland. More than once, he broke off his tours, canceled concerts, and fled back home. Then, after returning, he would immediately become anxious for a new journey. At home he worked obsessively. In addition to composition he started a new project—the exhausting and labourious proofreading of his works. His aim was to correct and clean everything, a task the composer's brother Modest described as "[like] preparations for a long journey when one is worried about what lies ahead but no less about what he abandons; [he] is anxious to finish the unfinished and set right all that is remediable." On the occasion of the newly corrected edition of his Third Suite, Tchaikovsky wrote Jurgenson: "When all my best pieces are published just like this one, I can die quietly." In late 1891 Tchaikovsky drew up his will. He feared for the fate of those closest to him in case of his death, particularly his nephew Vladimir Davidov. All of these emotions within him found their most brilliant embodiment in the final, outstanding creation of Tchaikovsky—his Sixth "Pathétique" Symphony (dedicated to Vladimir Davidov)—the highest peak of his creative genius, and which occupied him during the last months of his life.

The world glory of Tchaikovsky by then had become triumphal. He was elected a Corresponding Member of the French Academy. The University of Cambridge invited him to accept the degree of Doctor of Music—"Honoris Causa." At Cambridge, Tchaikovsky again met Walter Damrosch.

WALTER DAMROSCH TO PETER TCHAIKOVSKY

Buntings, Axbridge, England
July 30, 1893

My dear Mr. Tchaikovsky,

It gave me great pleasure to see you again in Cambridge and I truly regret that we were together for such a short time.

Your new symphony is awaited with great interest and I would like to know from you whether it will be published soon enough to perform it in New York during the current season. To tell the truth I hope to have the honor to premier it in America if it doesn't happen that you yourself will perform it here.

It would be impossible for you to find admirers more enthusiastic than the ones you have in America, who for this reason await each product of your genius with impatience.

Since you have always been very amiable towards me, you will be pleased to know that my opera is already well advanced, and that I hope to finish it before Christmas.

I shall remain here, in England until middle September and would be very grateful to you for a few words about your Symphony.

Ever yours,
Walter Damrosch

In Petersburg on October 28, 1893, Tchaikovsky conducted his final concert—the premier of his Sixth "Pathétique" Symphony. By Tchaikovsky's invitation, the pianist Adele Aus der Ohe participated in the concert. She performed Tchaikovsky's First Piano Concerto under the composer's direction again just as she had done in America when their acquaintance began. On November 1 Tchaikovsky suddenly fell ill and on the sixth he died. The sudden death of Tchaikovsky evoked a number of rumors and attracted attention to the most intimate aspects of his life. The official account of Tchaikovsky's death ascribed the cause to cholera and it was confirmed by his doctors and relatives. *However, some unofficial versions arose which were based on Tchaikovsky's alleged homosexuality and, in particular, his homosexual relations with the Tsar's court. According to one such account, an ad hoc court of the School of Jurisprudence in Petersburg, concerned with the honor of the school's name, sentenced its alumnus Tchaikovsky to death. In order to obey this brutal decree, the sensitive genius supposedly took poison. Another account accused Modest of poisoning Tchaikovsky in response to Alexander III's threat to defame the composer and exile him from Russia. In all of Tchaikovsky's vast published epistolary legacy, including more than 5000 letters and ten diaries, there is no reference to either his homosexuality or to the events leading to his sudden death. Nevertheless, the unofficial accounts are disturbing and can not be dismissed lightly because there exists the very real possibility of censorship by Modest, the founder of the Tchaikovsky museum in Klin and the author of a three-volume biography of the composer. It is possible, therefore, that certain documents are still preserved in the secret archives of the Tchaikovsky museum or have been destroyed. In any case the existence itself of these tales is indicative of how tumultuous the last years of Tchaikovsky's life actually were. The sad news of Tchaikovsky's death traveled with lightning speed to New York, where the next day Walter Damrosch gave an interview to reporters—in the Music Hall itself:*

(From Musical Courier, November 8, 1893)

I met Tchaikovsky in this country two years ago and I was charmed with his modesty, courtesy and graciousness of character. He was the most modest composer I ever met. I saw him again in Cambridge, England last summer in June, when he was one of five great composers from five different countries to receive the honorary degree of Doctor of Music. He seemed to be very glad to meet someone from America again, and told me that of all his musical experiences his visit to America had been the most harmonious, without discordant note to mar it. He spoke of the superb playing of the orchestra and, as he said, of the amiability of the chorus of the Oratorio Society in following his beat, although he claimed to be a very inexperienced chorus conductor.

At the banquet given that evening by the University in King's College I had the good luck to find my seat next to his. We exchanged many reminiscences of his visit to America and he promised me to come again next year. He was also good enough to promise me the first production of his new Symphony No. 6, of which he was then finishing the instrumentation and for the plan of which he gave me the outlines.

Russia loses in him her greatest national composer. He had an almost morbid fear that his compositions were showing signs of advancing age, and he was as pleased as a child when I told him that the American verdict of his last Symphony (No. 5) was that it was his greatest and most mature work. His music is always national in character. He uses the folk songs of Russia as a basis. He is much more distinctively a Russian national than Rubinstein, who was his master in composition, and he possessed to a much greater degree than Rubinstein a self critical faculty. His instrumentation is always brilliant, forcible and characteristic; his melodic themes strong; dramatic and passionate. He should not have died. He would have enriched the world by many masterpieces, as his intellect and creative faculties were in their prime.

From My Musical Life, by Walter Damrosch

In the spring of 1891 Carnegie Hall, which had been built by Andrew Carnegie as a home for the higher musical activities of New York, was inaugurated with a music festival in which the New York Symphony and Oratorio Societies took part. In order to give this festival a special significance, I invited Peter Ilyich Tchaikovsky, the great Russian composer, to come to America and to conduct some of his own works. In all my many years of experience I have never met a great composer so gentle, so modest—almost diffident—as he. We all loved him from the first moment—my wife and I, the chorus, the orchestra, the employees of the hotel where he lived, and of course, the public. He was not a conductor by profession and in consequence the technique of it, the rehearsals and concerts, fatigued him excessively; but he knew what he wanted and the atmosphere which emanated from him was so sympathetic and love-compelling that all executants strove with double eagerness to divine his intentions and to carry them out. The performance which he conducted of his Third Suite, for instance, was admirable, although it is in parts very difficult; and as he was virtually the first of great living composers to visit America, the public received him with jubilance.

He came often to our house, and, I think, liked to come. He was always gentle in his intercourse with others, but a feeling of sadness seemed never to leave him, although his reception in America was more than enthusiastic and the visit so successful in every way that he made plans to come back the following year. Yet he was often swept by uncontrollable waves of melancholia and despondency.

The following year in May I went to England with my wife, and received an invitation from Charles Villiers Stanford, then professor of music at Cambridge, to visit the old university during the interesting commencement exercises at which honorary degrees of Doctor of Music were to be given to five composers of five different countries—Saint-Saens, of France, Boito of Italy, Grieg of Norway, Bruch of Germany, and Tchaikovsky of Russia.

In the evening a great banquet was given in the refectory of the college, and by good luck I was placed next to Tchaikovsky. He told me during the dinner that he had just finished a new symphony which was different in form from any he had ever written. I asked him in what the difference consisted and he answered: "The last movement is an adagio and the whole work has a programme."

"Do tell me the programme," I demanded eagerly.

"No," he said, "that I shall never tell. But I shall send you the first orchestral score and parts as soon as Jurgenson, my publisher, has them ready." We parted with the expectation of meeting again in America during the following winter, but, alas, in November came the cable announcing his death from cholera, and a few days later arrived a package from Moscow containing the score and parts of his Symphony No. 6, the "Pathetique." It was like a message from the dead. I immediately put the work into rehearsal and gave it its first performance in America on the following Sunday. Its success was immediate and profound. We gave it many repetitions that winter and I have played it since in concerts all over the United States. Other orchestras have cultivated it with equal assiduity. . . .

Notes

Introduction

1 After the Russian Revolution of 1917, Tchaikovsky was surnamed a "narrow-minded whimperer"; his music was diagnosed as decadent, dissonant to the Revolution, and therefore useless to the people. Only gradually was this vulgarization overcome. Even now the change in official opinion is not complete; nevertheless, Tchaikovsky remains one of the Russian people's most beloved composers.

I. The Invitation

2 Leopold Damrosch is thought to be the first performer of Tchaikovsky's Violin Concerto (as a soloist accompanied by piano) in New York in 1879. This is based on the date in N. F. von Meck's letter to Tchaikovsky of December 27, 1881: "And now I see that Damrosch played your Concerto two years ago in New York. What a brave fellow! The Lord give us more such men!"

3 There was a party at Tchaikovsky's home in Frolovskoe on January 20 and 21, attended by his friends, including the composer Arensky, pianists Ziloty and Zverev, Jurgenson, and the music writer Laroche.

4 *Symphony*, a play by Modest Ilyich (Modia) Tchaikovsky (1850–1916), the younger brother of Peter Tchaikovsky, lawyer, playwright, and author of a three-volume biography of P. Tchaikovsky.

5 Tchaikovsky gave monetary support to Nikolai Peresleny (Kokodes), his young relative.

6 Medeia Figner (scheduled to play Lisa), wife of the Imperial Opera soloist Nikolay (playing Herman), was pregnant.

7 Tchaikovsky's concert in Paris took place on April 5, 1891, with the Colonne Orchestra under the direction of the composer.

8 Ivan Alexandrovich Vsevolozhsky, the head of the Imperial Theater Directorate.

9 Charles F. Tretbar, the representative of the Steinway Piano Company in New York.

10 Nicholas De Giers, Russian statesman of Swedish extraction, the minister of foreign affairs in the government of Alexander III.

11 The world premier of the Piano Concerto No. 1 was held in Boston on October 25, 1875, with Hans von Bülow as soloist.

12 Konstantin Konstantinovich Romanov, Grand Duke, cousin of Alexander III, poet, and amateur composer.

13 "Confiturenbourg," the opening scene of the second act of the *Nutcracker* ballet.

14 *Novoe Vremya*, Petersburg daily newspaper.

I I. *Twenty-five Days in America*

15 Francis Hyde, President of the New York Philharmonic Society, and the Trust Company Bank.

16 Knabe Piano Company, Baltimore, Maryland.

17 The correspondent mistook Morris Reno's daughter Alice for Tchaikovsky's wife.

18 Anton Rubinstein (1829–1894), Russian composer and one of the world's greatest pianists. In 1862 he founded the Petersburg Conservatory. Rubinstein toured America in 1872–73, giving 215 concerts.

19 Tchaikovsky completed the letter-diary to Modest Tchaikovsky on his passage to America and wrote the letter to Anatoly and Pania Tchaikovsky.

20 Alexander Nikolayevich Ostrovsky (1823–1886), notable Russian playwright.

21 Young Thomas, the son of the conductor Theodore Thomas.

22 Max Vogrich (1852–1916), Austrian-American composer.

23 Peter Sergeyevich Botkin, the secretary of the Russian embassy in Washington, son of the great Russian doctor-scientist S. P. Botkin.

24 Tchaikovsky's letters of April 29, 1891 are yet to be found.

25 Nikolai Rubinstein (1835–1881), pianist, conductor, founder of the Moscow Conservatory in 1863, brother of Anton Rubinstein.

26 Eduard Francevich Napravnik (1839–1916), Russian conductor and composer, the Music Director of the Petersburg Imperial Opera Theater.

27 "No, only he who knew" are the beginning words of Tchaikovsky's song, "None but the Lonely Heart."

28 "Red Sarafan," a popular Russian folk song.

29 Anton Seidl (1850–1898), eminent conductor, student at the Leipzig Conservatory, assistant to Wagner in Bayreuth, Music Director of the German Opera and Philharmonic Society in New York.

30 Tchaikovsky's opera, *The Maid of Orleans (Joan of Arc)* was not performed in New York at that time. The first performance of this opera in America took place in 1979 by the Michigan Opera Theater in Detroit.

31 Nikolay Conrady, deaf and dumb pupil of Modest Tchaikovsky.

32 Anna Petrovna Merkling (1830–1911), Tchaikovsky's cousin.

33 Julius Conius (1869–1942), violinist, friend of Tchaikovsky.

34 Leon Margulis, Morris Reno's son-in-law and secretary.

35 Antonia Mielke, a leading soprano of the New York Metropolitan Opera.

36 The Russian heir Nikolay (Tsar Nikolay II to be) was on a major trip to the Far East. A Japanese policeman attacked Nikolay with his sword. Although the heir received one blow on the forehead, he was not seriously injured.

37 During this time the competition among piano manufacturers was very keen. Between the Midwest and East Coast there existed as many as fifty different piano companies. The New York weekly magazine, *Musical Courier,* carried advertisements for all of the companies. In the May 20, 1891 issue, the magazine published this brief message: "Although Mr. Peter Tchaikovsky is not a piano virtuoso we would not be surprised to find his name attached to a piano testimonial on an American piano before he gets through with his American experiences. And it is all right, too, for Mr. Tchaikovsky is in many respects a better judge of a piano than some pianists."

III. *To America Again?*

38 Tchaikovsky never completed this symphony but used the material for his Third Piano Concerto in E-flat Major.

39 Alexander Ziloty (1863–1945), pianist, conductor, and pupil of Nikolay Rubinstein and Peter Tchaikovsky.

40 Letters from Tchaikovsky to the Reno family are yet to be found.

41 Jakov Stepanovich Kalishevsky, Music Director of the men's and boys' chorus of the Sofiysky Cathedral in Kiev.

42 See note 34.

43 Afanasy Afanasyevich Fet (1820–1892), notable Russian lyric poet.

44 Tchaikovsky tore up the score of *Voevoda* after its first performance in Moscow on November 6, 1891, with the words: "Such garbage should not be written." Later, under the supervision of Alexander Ziloty, the score was restored in accordance with the orchestral parts.

45 Mikhail Mikhailovich Ippolitov-Ivanov (1859–1935), Russian composer and conductor.

Index